Details in Architecture

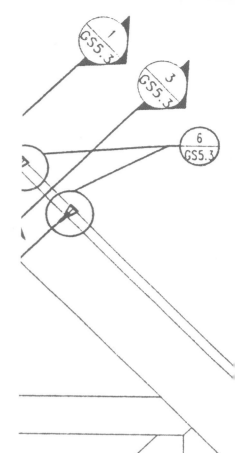

Details in Architecture

Creative Detailing

by some of the World's

Leading Architects

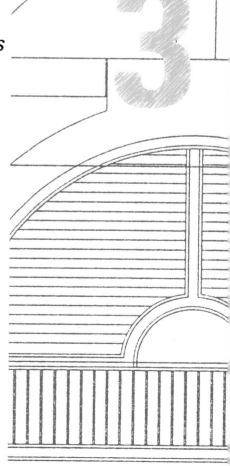

69494

First published in Australia in 2001 by
The Images Publishing Group Pty Ltd
ABN 89 059 734 431
6 Bastow Place, Mulgrave, Victoria, 3170, Australia
Telephone: +61 3 9561 5544 Facsimile: +61 3 9561 4860
email: books@images.com.au
website: www.imagespublishing.com.au

Copyright © The Images Publishing Group Pty Ltd
The Images Publishing Group Reference Number: 420

National Library of Australia
Cataloguing-in-Publication data

Details in Architecture 3: Creative Detailing by some of the
World's Leading Architects

ISBN: 1 86470 093 9

1. Architecture – Details. 2. Decoration and ornament,
Architectural.

721

Designed by The Graphic Image Studio Pty Ltd,
Mulgrave, Australia
Printed in Hong Kong

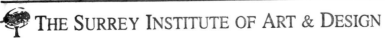

CONTENTS

CONTENTS

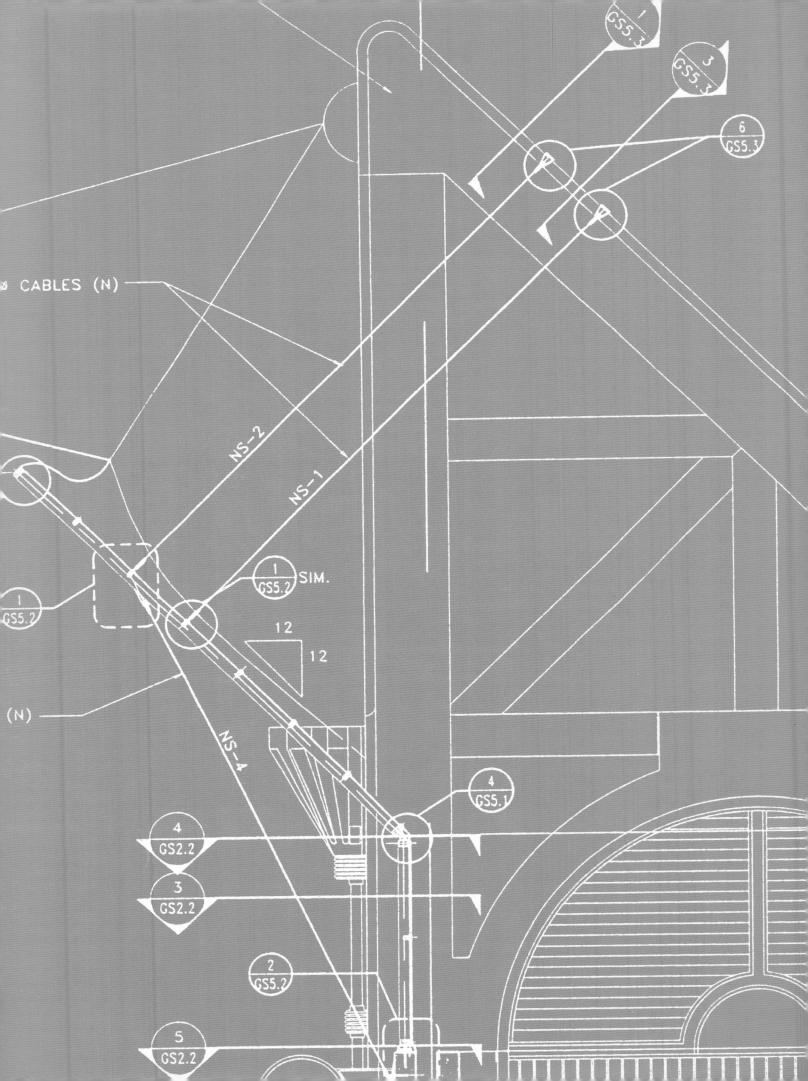

It could be said that detail fuses a relationship between matter and ourselves and is therefore fundamental to human existence.

Prior to using cameras, architectural detail was, of necessity, linked together with matter: for instance, in Europe it was critical to have the detailed form of stone correct before it was cut and stacked, while in Japan the detailed finish on the corners of a wooden pillar and the cupola between a pillar and a crossbeam were perceived to be as important as the function of the architecture itself.

Photography changed this relationship between detail and ourselves in that architecture came to exist in two dimensions, with detail being seen principally as a tool to shape the edge of a form.

Today, however, the meaning of detail is beginning to revert to its previous state with the function of the building being understood to be as important as its form, and the architectural detail used to define the function viewed as fundamental to the function itself.

—*Kengo Kuma* (Kengo Kuma & Associates, Tokyo, Japan)

SKYLIGHT

REPUBLIC OF SINGAPORE YACHT CLUB, REPUBLIC OF SINGAPORE
Alfred Wong Partnership Pte Ltd

1

1 Interior showing skylight
2 Skylight section
3 Plan of skylight
Photography: Albert Lam

The main circulation areas in the recently completed Republic of Singapore Yacht Club are open sided and so naturally ventilated. This skylight is one of a pair that share typical details. It is located over the main staircase connecting the two primary floors of the club. The detail has proved to be simple and effective.

The skylight has been treated as a flat plane of glass suspended over the elliptical aperture. The edge of the glass extends well beyond the opening to minimise the ingress of rainwater, and the gap between the underside and the upstands facilitates the venting of warm air from within the building.

The steel supporting structure has been detailed to evoke the tectonic imagery of both traditional and contemporary boat construction.

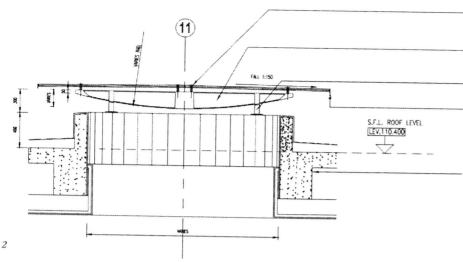

Skylight formed in four laminated glass panels point supported in locations indicated

MS Beams of varying lengths formed with lower flange to radius and boxing within the web as indicated. To be ground smooth and finished with colour

75mm diameter support to MS beam. Stainless steel finish

Drip formed in 3x30mm natural anodised aluminium curved to radii

RC to structural engineer's detail

S.F.L. ROOF LEVEL
LEV.110.400

FALL 1:150

2

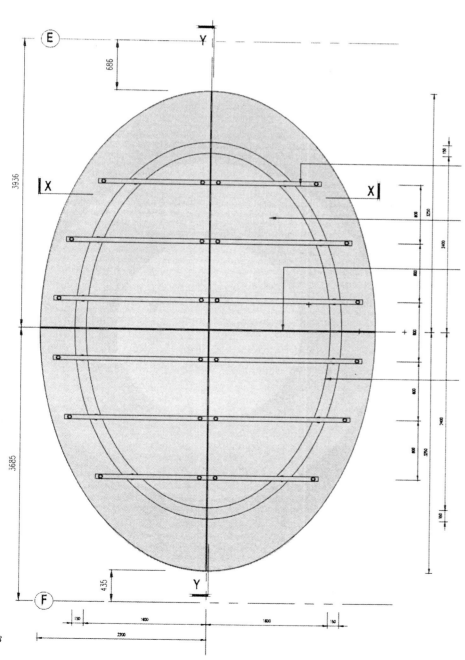

MS beams of varying lengths formed with lower flange to radius and boxing within the web as indicated. To be ground smooth and finished with colour

Skylight formed with laminated glass panels – point supported in locations indicated
Glass to be blue/green, semi-reflective with 30 per cent dot matrix silk screen applied ceramic fit

Glass panels to be butt joined with approved clear silicon sealant drip formed in 3x330mm natural anodised curved to radii

3

11

PORCH ROOF AND COLUMN

BMW DRIVING CENTER, BORNEM, BELGIUM
ARCHI+I SPRL, Architecture

1

1   Covering steel plate d440/10mm
2   Steel column d457/25mm
3   Strengthening steel ring d504/20mm
4   Connection plate 35mm
5   Tie beam M42
6   Aluminium lagging 2mm
7   Tie beam M36
8   IPE 400
9   Tie beam 80x80x3mm
10 Drainpipe d110 – 2cm/m

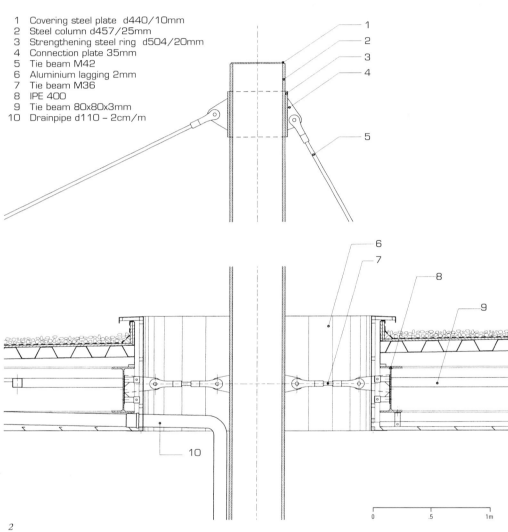

2

1   *Structural elements*
2   *Column detail*
3   *Porch roof section*
4   *Porch roof*
5   *Column detail*
Photography: Ch. Bastin & J. Evrard

The program for the BMW Driving Center, a pilot project for the BMW AG Group, has two clearly defined sections; a showroom to welcome the customers in a real and virtual BMW-world and a covered area where the test-cars are shown and picked up. Both areas of the building have been conceived in a steel structure, the showroom in a more 'classical' way with beams and columns.

The partly open shed, suspended by cables on 10 pillars with a height of eight metres, is floating 6.4 metres above the ground. The concept of the structure is accentuated by cut-outs around the pillars and a rectangular cut-out in the middle.

The shed reflects an interaction between solids and voids, height and mass, with different perceptions from different points of view.

The execution process dealt with the limits of the transport and the limited construction time (20 days on-site). All materials have been chosen for their reduced maintenance cost and timeless character.

As an attraction point for the company, the structure and building reflect the technicality, fine design and transparency of the BMW AG Group.

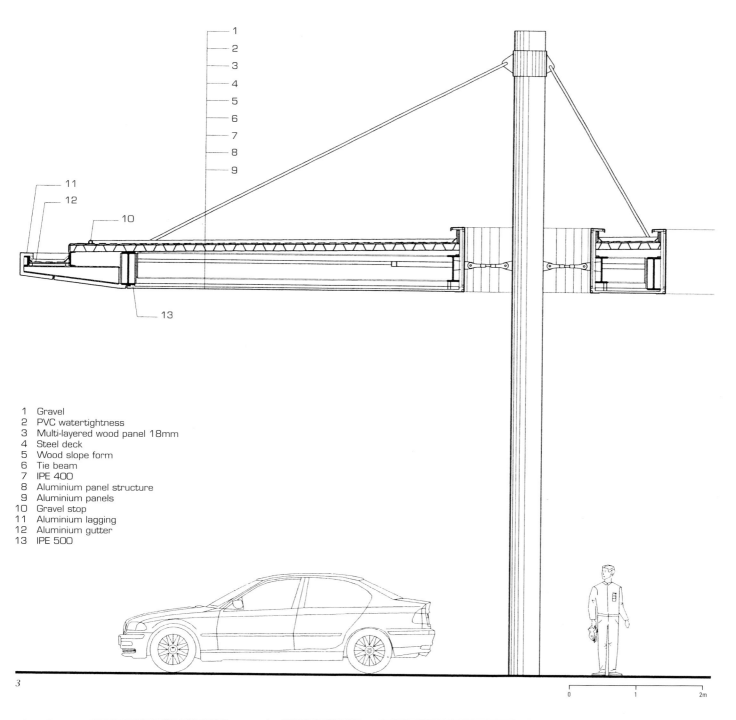

1 Gravel
2 PVC watertightness
3 Multi-layered wood panel 18mm
4 Steel deck
5 Wood slope form
6 Tie beam
7 IPE 400
8 Aluminium panel structure
9 Aluminium panels
10 Gravel stop
11 Aluminium lagging
12 Aluminium gutter
13 IPE 500

3

0   1   2m

4

5

CANOPY AND SUNSCREENS
MINISTRY OF FOREIGN AFFAIRS, BANGKOK, THAILAND
Architects 49 Limited

1

1   *Front façade showing canopy*
2   *Canopy section*
3   *Canopy front elevation*
4&6 *Detail of canopy structural connection*
5   *Canopy side elevation*

Architectural details have been developed for this government building located in tropical Thailand. The design includes a canopy, which has been positioned above the main entrance to the banquet hall, sunshades and a pediment.

The curved lines of the canopy and the simple straight-line form of the building initially seemed a contradiction. The finish of the canopy is stainless steel with an insertion of laminated glass and dotted film that dramatically defuses the sunlight to the porch below. The details of structural connections and supports have been modified in order to conform with the design concept, creating the effect of simplicity but attractiveness.

Similarly, the outside panels of the building have been installed with sunscreens. The function of the screens is to reduce heat and the penetration of direct sunlight into the building. The sunscreen also functions as a catwalk for cleaning and maintenance of the façade and windows. The figure of the screen has been modelled on a lotus flower, which is the symbol of Thailand's Ministry of Foreign Affairs.

The maintenance of the building influenced the selection of materials for the sunscreens. They are made from stainless steel with the oval component made from aluminium. The screens have been

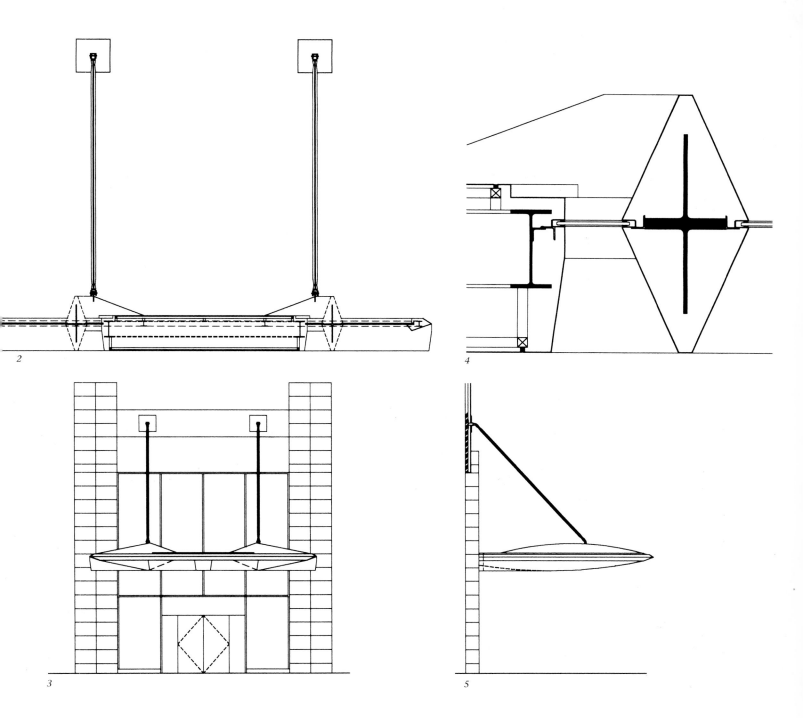

2

4

3

5

designed on a modular system with a nut and bolt connection system. The metal plate has been installed along with the dry process, granite panel installation. The essential point is that the plates can be adjusted to ensure that the lines of the screen are horizontal.

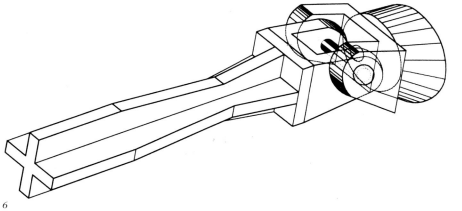

6

7

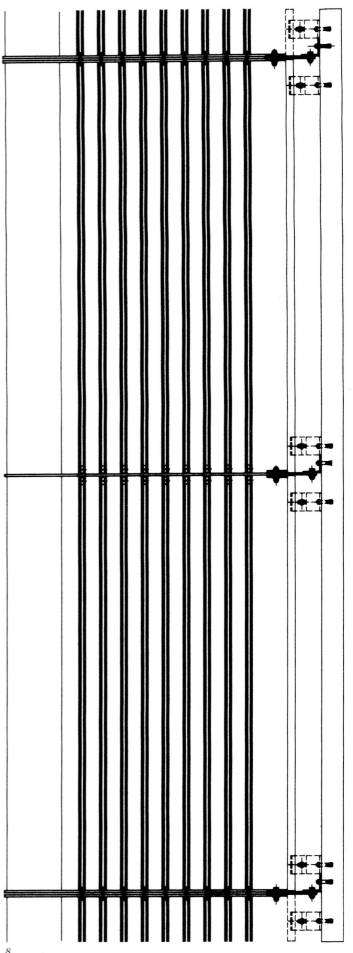

8

7&9 *Façade of building showing sunshades*
8 *Plan of sunshade*
10 *Section of sunshade*
Photography: Skyline Studio

9

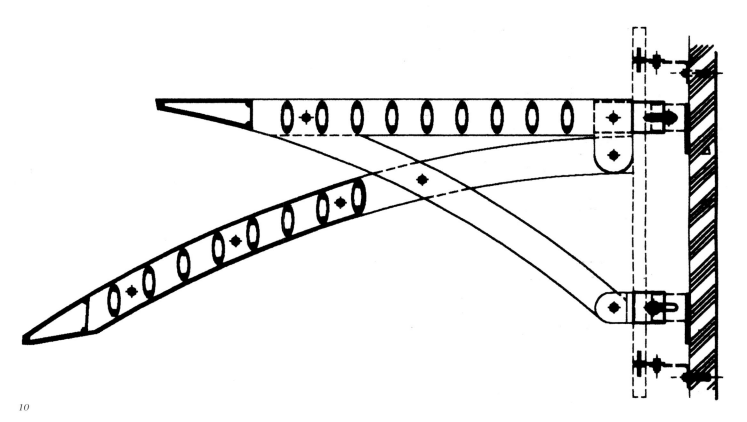

10

STAIRS, MEETING AREA AND RECEPTION

BENFIELD GREIG, LONDON, UK
Austin-Smith:Lord

1

2

1   Glass staircase
2   Glass staircase viewed from above
3&4 Details of glass staircase
5   Fourth floor reception area featuring
    curved video wall

The refurbishment of this 6,875-square-metre office space included the installation of a new staircase to unite three open-plan floors and facilitate better communication between staff, new meeting rooms and a reception area.

The staircase has been designed to be an object of interest, but not to be physically or visually obtrusive. The stairs consist of two concentric steel box sections which form semi-circular cranked spiral beams spanning between floors. A single intermediate suspension rod at mid-span on each level simplifies the load transfer at the main floor connections and controlled vibration.

The stairs were fabricated off-site, cut into sections for delivery and reassembly, and welded in-situ. Drama has been added with a judicious use of colours uplighting the elegant stair.

The new reception has been set back from the lifts and angled at 45 degrees. It is a mixture of birds eye maple, glass and steel, with specially designed uplights striped with copper and aluminium leaf. The desk is backed by a 6.25-metre projection screen, reflecting images of the Benfield Greig business and providing a constantly changing backdrop.

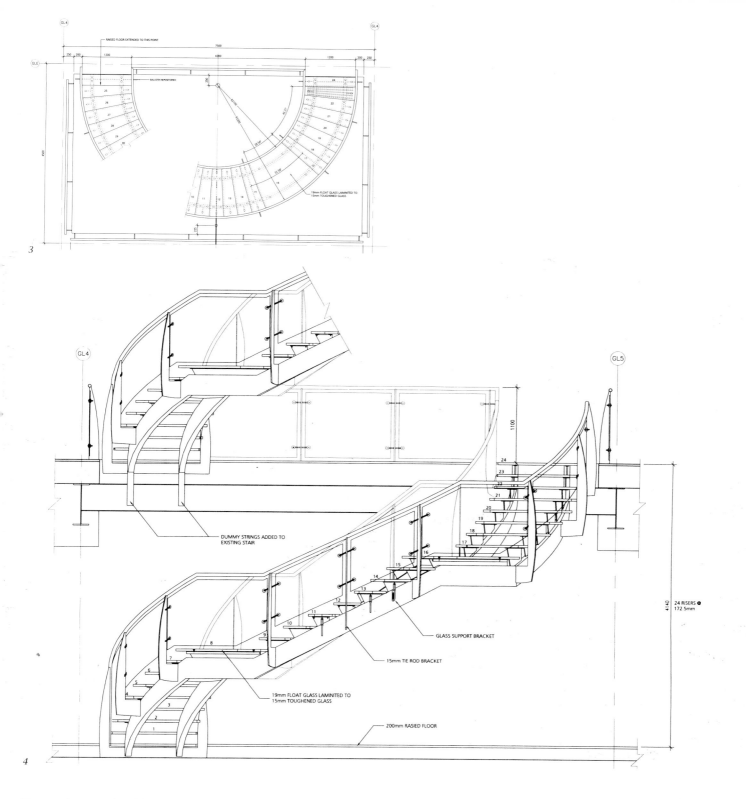

3

4

DUMMY STRINGS ADDED TO
EXISTING STAIR

GLASS SUPPORT BRACKET

15mm TIE ROD BRACKET

19mm FLOAT GLASS LAMINITED TO
15mm TOUGHENED GLASS

200mm RASIED FLOOR

19mm FLOAT GLASS LAMINITED TO
15mm TOUGHENED GLASS

RAISED FLOOR EXTENDED TO THIS POINT

BALUSTRE REPOSITIONED

24 RISERS @
172.5mm

The meeting areas, 'snails', were developed as part of the design meeting concept. The staff work in a predominantly open environment and meeting spaces were required to cater to a variety of needs from 'five-minute' informal chats to formal board meetings. The concept has been designed to give individuality to the rooms or spaces and help set the mood for the meeting. Meeting areas are available to all staff on a booking system. The name 'snail' was derived from the wraparound cocoon nature of the glass enclosure.

5

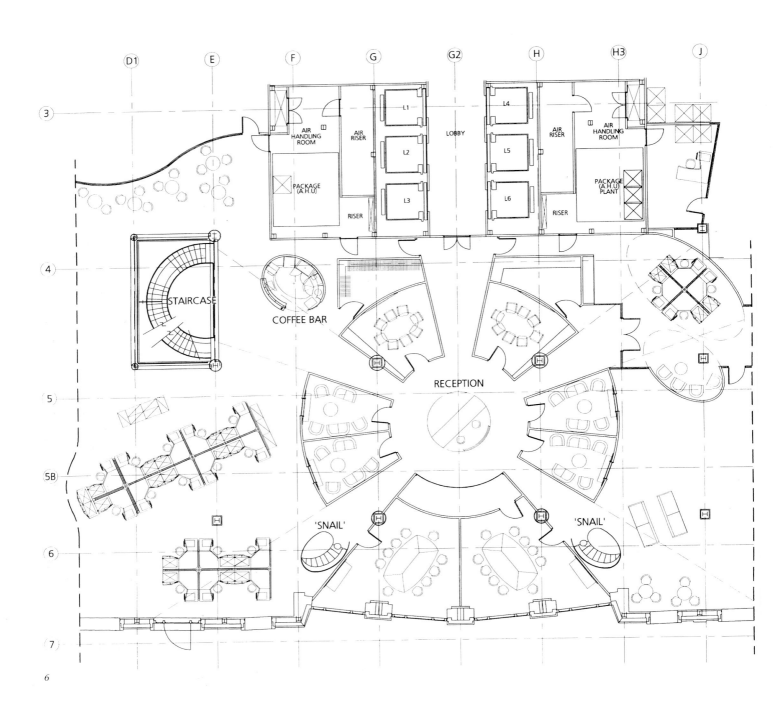

STAIRCASE

COFFEE BAR

RECEPTION

'SNAIL'

'SNAIL'

AIR HANDLING ROOM

AIR RISER

PACKAGE (A.H.U)

RISER

LOBBY

L1

L2

L3

L4

L5

L6

AIR RISER

AIR HANDLING ROOM

PACKAGE (A.H.U) PLANT

RISER

6

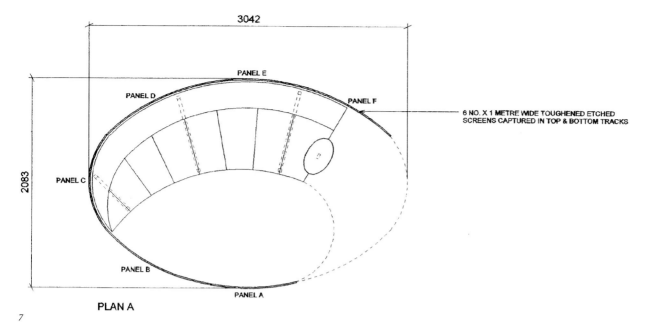

3042

2083

PANEL E

PANEL D

PANEL F

PANEL C

PANEL B

PANEL A

PLAN A

6 NO. X 1 METRE WIDE TOUGHENED ETCHED
SCREENS CAPTURED IN TOP & BOTTOM TRACKS

7

6   Detailed plan of fourth floor reception area
7   Detail of 'snail' – informal meeting area
8   Interior of glass 'snail' meeting area
Photography: Philip Vile Photography

8

CANOPY
QUEEN STREET MALL CENTRAL STRUCTURE, BRISBANE, AUSTRALIA
Bligh Voller Nield Pty Ltd

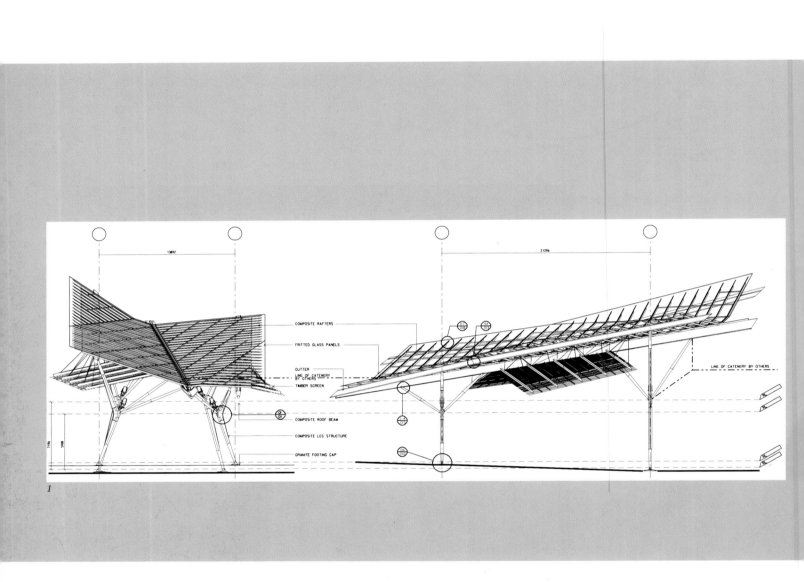

COMPOSITE RAFTERS

FRITTED GLASS PANELS

GUTTER
LINE OF CATENERY
BY OTHERS

TIMBER SCREEN

LINE OF CATENERY BY OTHERS

COMPOSITE ROOF BEAM

COMPOSITE LEG STRUCTURE

GRANITE FOOTING CAP

1

The Brisbane City Council obtained a great deal of advice from various groups for the development of the Queen Street Mall. The design responds to urban and street geometries, and includes a line in the centre of the mall that organises and groups a variety of structures that accommodate uses from cafes and restaurants to stages, catwalks and stairs to the underground bus station. The centrepiece of this urban assembly is the angled line of the structure that allows a new order in the mall while providing space and access for emergency vehicles and servicing.

Embracing the glancing geometries and ordered by the design principles is a diverse family of structures in a new Queensland language of architecture. The roofing is a sloping translucent polycarbonate with layers supported by fabricated steel beams and circular columns. The roof is a play of translucency, light, shade, permeability and frame. Many structures have two roofs; a weather roof and a secondary roof for shading

The columns have been restrained by braces, reducing the structural size. The central structure

2

3

4

1   *Elevation of canopies*
2–4   *View of canopy structure*

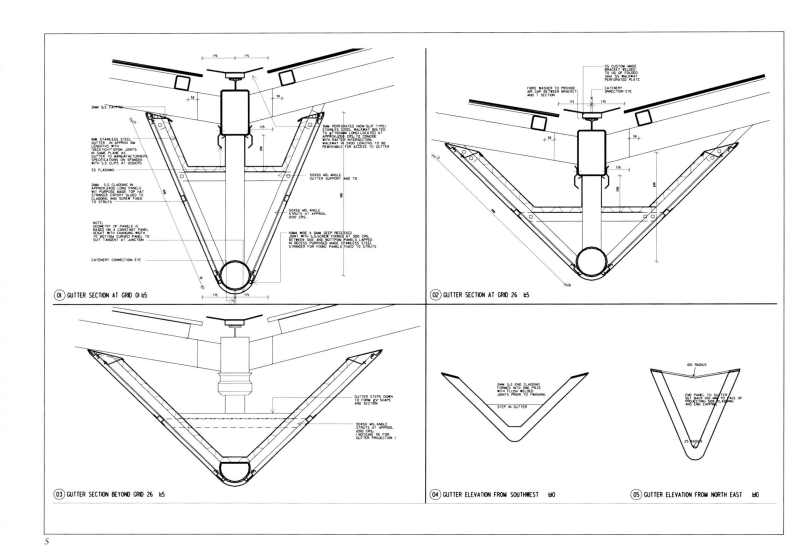

uses a different language of shaped tubular columns holding up the glass weather and timber shade roof. This is a purpose-built and integrated structure as opposed to the range and variety of the kit-of-parts used in the smaller structures. A shift of materials from polycarbonate to glass signals that this has a special urban role. It contrasts with the variety and vitality of the Polyglass and steel with its added humanity.

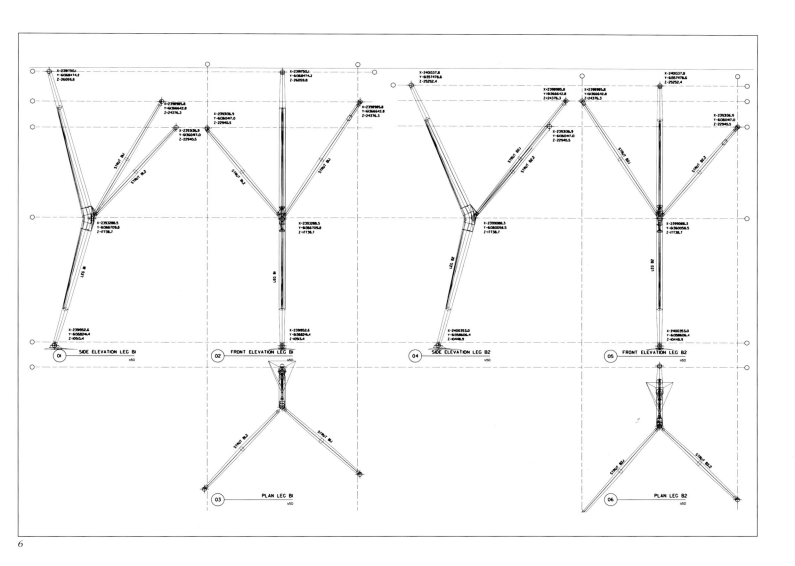

6

7

5   Gutter sections
6   Side and front elevations
7   View of gutter
Photography: David Sandison

FOOTBRIDGES
RETAIL AREA, CENTRO EMPRESARIAL NAÇÕES UNIDAS (CENU), SÃO PAULO, BRAZIL
Botti Rubin Arquitetos Associados

1

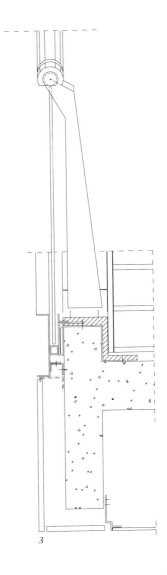

3

1 Footbridge
2 Retail area
3 Detail of lateral handrail
4 Detail of structural supports and handrail
5&6 Section of anchorage
7 Plan and section of footbridge
8 Underview of footbridge
Photography: Tuca Reinés

2

The three CENU towers (two office buildings and a 506-room hotel) contain underground retail outlets and restaurants. The commercial area extends below ground under the buildings, however the 15-metre-high central spans of the sky roof ensure natural light and a view.

The foot bridges permit pedestrian circulation on the higher retail level. These bridges were built with the same three-dimensional structural system used for the roof. The floors are made of translucent 36-millimetre glass, and the handrails are made of aluminium tubes, which are fitted over transparent 20-millimetre tempered glass.

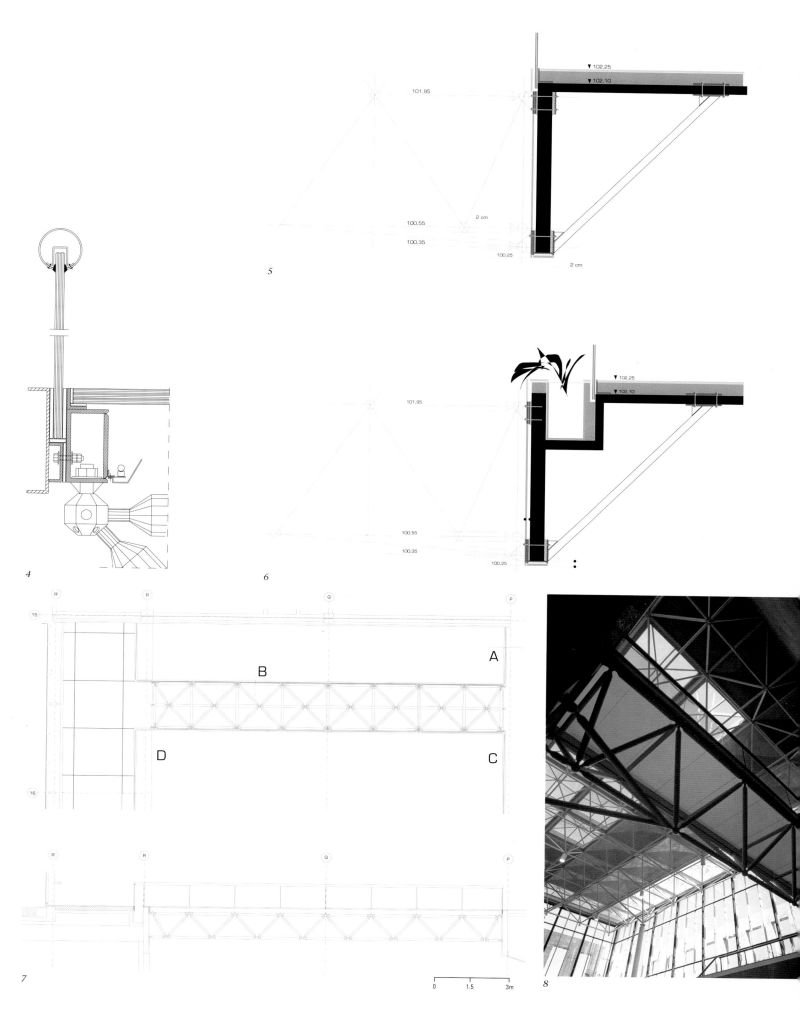

4

5

6

101.95

100.55

100.35

100.25

2 cm

2 cm

▼ 102,25

▼ 102,10

101.95

100.55

100.35

100.25

▼ 102,25

▼ 102,10

7

A

B

D

C

R'   R   Q   P

15

16

R'   R   Q   P

8

0   1.5   3m

GLASS CANOPIES
CENU NORTH & WEST TOWERS, OF THE CENTRO EMPRESARIAL NAÇÕES UNIDAS, SÃO PAULO, BRAZIL
Botti Rubin Arquitetos Associados

1

3

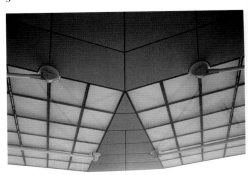

4

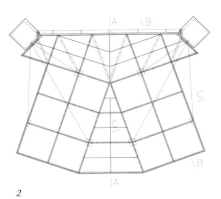

2

These two canopies cover the entrances of two office buildings that are part of the 275,000-square-metre three-tower CENU complex. The third building is a 506-room Hilton Hotel. Both canopies have been built using steel and aluminium frames holding double-layered translucent glass panels with fibre-optic lighting in between.

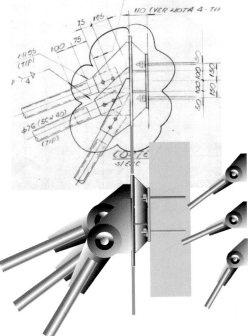

5

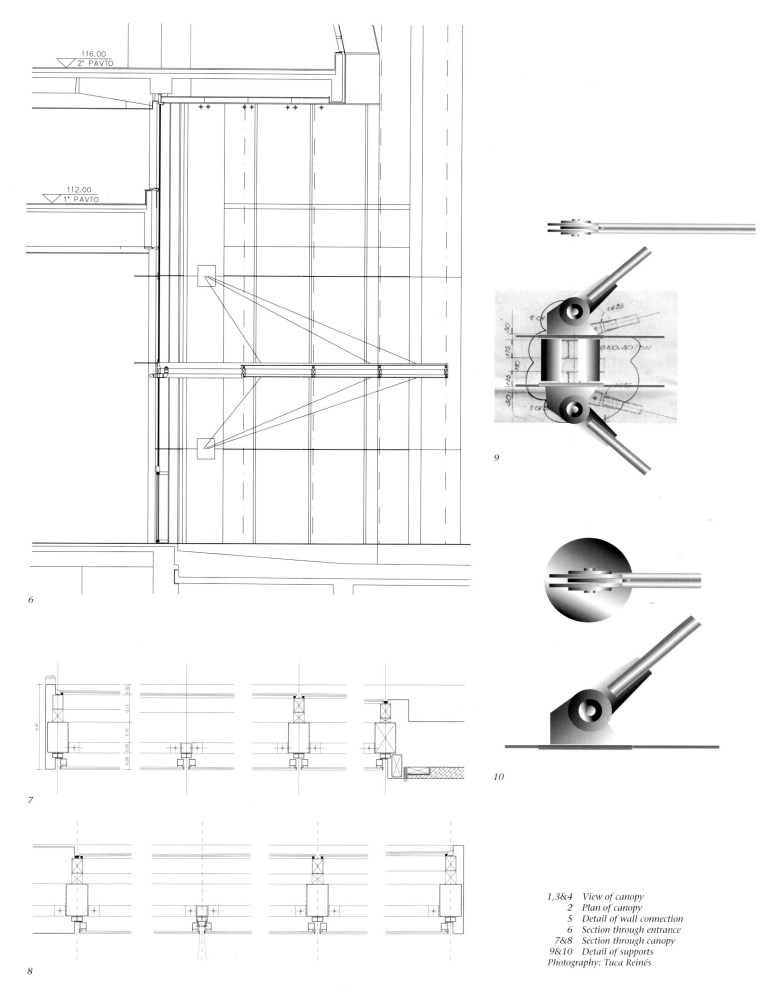

116.00
2° PAVTO

112.00
1° PAVTO

6

7

8

9

10

1,3&4   View of canopy
2   Plan of canopy
5   Detail of wall connection
6   Section through entrance
7&8   Section through canopy
9&10   Detail of supports
Photography: Tuca Reinés

ROOF STRUCTURE
CARLOS BRATKE'S RESIDENCE, AVENIDA OSCAR AMERICANO, SÃO PAULO, BRAZIL
Carlos Bratke Ateliê de arquitetura

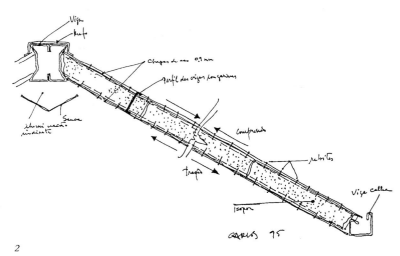

2

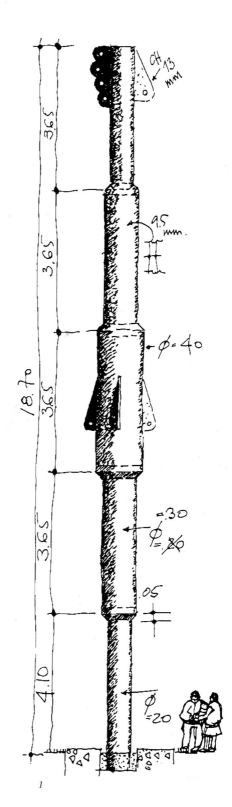

1

3

The inspiration for the design of this house was the idea of a house within a house.

The metallic roofing and its structural support function like an area built in the conventional fashion. However, the building lot has a four-metre decline from the street, which suggests an inversion of the traditional two-storey house. The living room is at street level, while the other rooms – the bedrooms – are on a lower level. This solves the problem of street noise quite satisfactorily.

The house is located on a very busy street, which is why special consideration was given to acoustic solutions, and why the façade facing the avenida is completely sealed by a 20-centimetre-thick concrete wall.

The roof structure of the house was selected to make it possible to deflect sound waves; the simplest of the solutions considered for the project.

1 Detail of mast
2 Roof detail
3&4 External view of roof structure and mast
5 Elevation
6 Mast
7 Detail fixing of pluvial water gutter in concrete column
8 View across pool to roof structure

Photography: Carolina Bratke

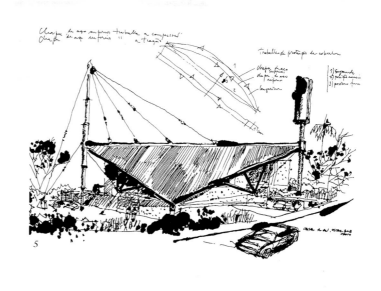

5

4

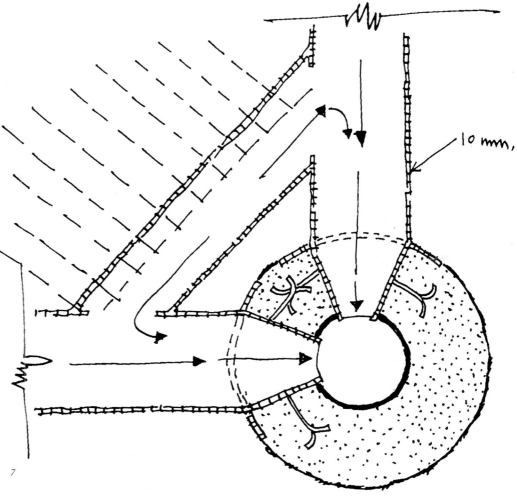
7

6

8

TRELLIS
CONSORCIO – VIDA BUILDING, SANTIAGO, CHILE
Enrique Browne & Associates, Architects in association with Chemetov + Huidobro, Architects

1

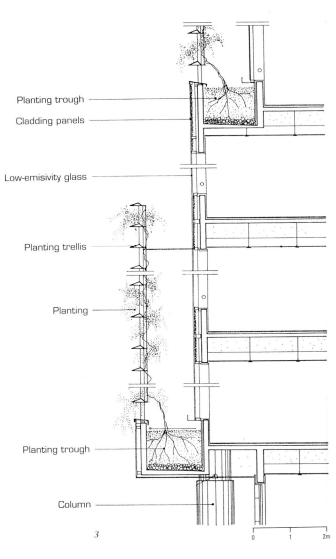

Planting trough

Cladding panels

Low-emisivity glass

Planting trellis

Planting

Planting trough

Column

3

0   1   2m

2

This office tower in Santiago, Chile features a trellised west-facing wall to filter the hot summer sun. The building has two main volumes, the principal volume having 16 levels and being 75-metres long.

The design incorporates both technical and natural methods to shelter the western façade. Thermo-panes have been included, and the exterior has been dressed with vegetation. The greenery of the western façade reduces the building's solar absorption, transforming it into a 3,200-square-metre vertical garden, enlivening the building and giving it a changing aspect during the different seasons.

The trellis is approximately 1.5 metres from the building to allow the façade cleaning machine to operate. The same device is used to give the gardener access to the plants. Large metal visors offer protection to the upper two floors of the building, as well as providing a finishing touch.

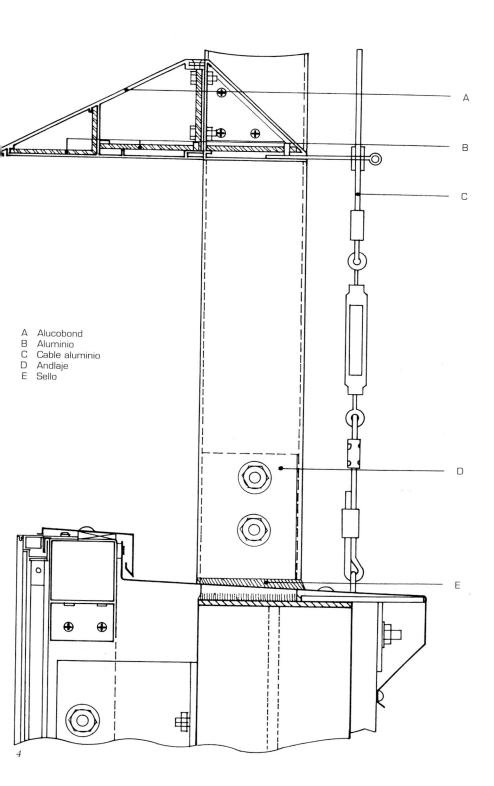

A   Alucobond
B   Aluminio
C   Cable aluminio
D   Andlaje
E   Sello

A

B

C

D

E

4

5

6

1   *View inside trellis*
2   *View of west-facing façade*
3   *Detail of vertical trellis*
4   *Vertical detail of trellis*
5   *View of west-facing façade*
6   *View from interior through trellis*
Photography: Enrique Browne (1), Guy Wenborne (2,5&6)

WATERFALL AND WINDMILL

WHEELWRIGHT RANCH, OAKLEY, UTAH, USA
Carol R. Johnson Associates, Inc.

1

1   Wall, cascade and watering trough
2   Cascade and watering trough plan
3   Cascade section elevation

The Wheelwright Ranch is a 17-hectare parcel of land set high above the Weber River in Oakley, Utah. Carol R. Johnson Associates, Inc. was retained by the owners at the beginning of the project to work with the architect in locating the home and designing the site and related structures. Open fields, new roadways and pathways were developed, and several new structures, including a grand entry drive, barn, bridle paths, paddocks, a windmill and pond were designed and built.

The design incorporates sustainable systems for water flow and wind power. Water drawn from the Weber River flows into the pond before cascading over a 'ha-ha' wall to a rock-lined horse watering trough, and is then returned to the river.

A windmill pumps aerated water back into the pond where it is recirculated through the system. Diversion valves were designed for water to be pumped to the upper fields to irrigate the 15 hectares of pasture and paddocks.

Native stone found on the site was used in the structures and landscape. The 'ha-ha' wall was built into a slope to corral the horses and preserve the views from the house across the fields. It was dry-laid using fractured stone blasted during excavation for the ponds and stream. River washed cobble sieved from the topsoil was used to face the bridge, veneer the house foundation and line the ponds and stream.

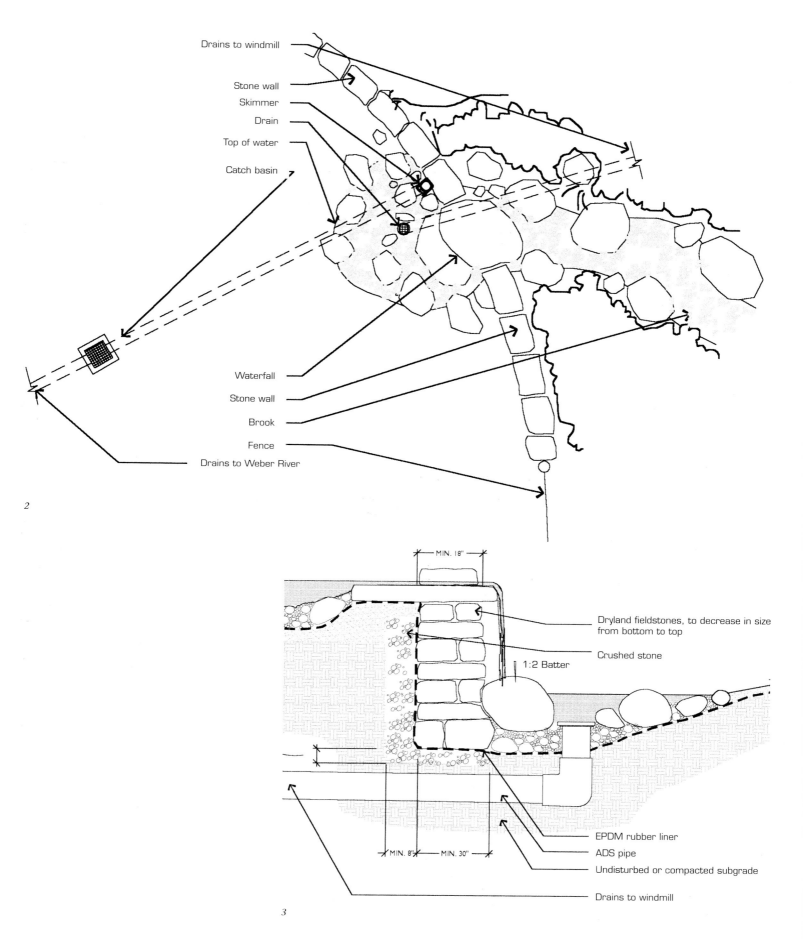

Drains to windmill

Stone wall

Skimmer

Drain

Top of water

Catch basin

Waterfall

Stone wall

Brook

Fence

Drains to Weber River

2

MIN. 18"

Dryland fieldstones, to decrease in size from bottom to top

Crushed stone

1:2 Batter

MIN. 8" — MIN. 30"

EPDM rubber liner

ADS pipe

Undisturbed or compacted subgrade

Drains to windmill

3

4

4   *View to house with pond, windmill and*
     bridge
5   *Windmill and pump elevation*
Photography: Jack Okland, Jr. & Company

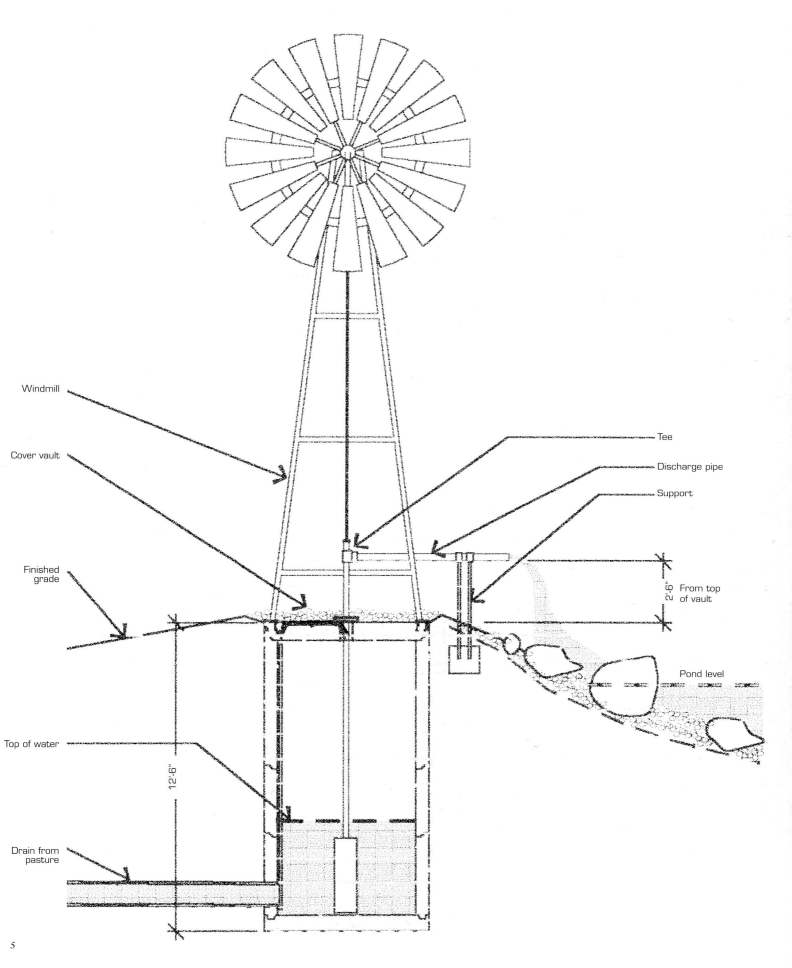

Windmill

Cover vault

Finished
grade

Top of water

Drain from
pasture

Tee

Discharge pipe

Support

2'-6" From top
of vault

Pond level

12'-6"

5

EXPOSED CONCRETE VAULTS

THE CONRAN SHOP, MARYLEBONE, LONDON, UK
Conran & Partners

1

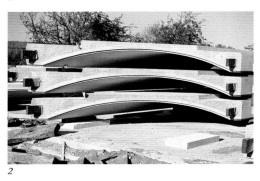

2

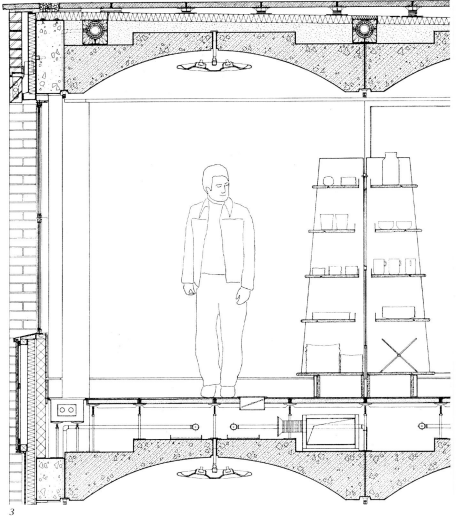

3

1   Installation of precast concrete units
2   Precast concrete unit
3   Detail section through shop and terrace
4   Typical bay
5   Sectional perspective through shop and
     restaurant
6   Detail junction of in-situ column and
     beam with precast bolt
Photography: Peter Cook (4&6), Mark
Fairhurst (1&2)

The construction of the Conran Shop behind the façade of the existing mews building on Marylebone High Street, London uses an exposed concrete structure to create a 'sophisticated warehouse' feel. It houses a contemporary department store selling a wide variety of designer merchandise.

The choice of exposed concrete structural vaults was conceived to act as an integrating element throughout the building, eliminating the typical serviced suspended ceiling normally associated with retail design.

To achieve a high-quality self finish, the concrete and mould were carefully specified with input from the manufacturer and engineer.

A single shot-blasted steel mould was chosen for all units. Due to the site geometry with the existing building, this mould was adapted to create the foreshortened units which kept the fabrication of moulds to a minimum, maintaining good economy.

A limestone aggregate and Portland cement were carefully chosen to create a chalky-white colour, avoiding the sometimes drab appearance of standard grey concrete.

To enable integration of services an accessible raised floor system was adopted. The penetrations in the slab were co-ordinated to allow supply to smoke detectors, sprinkler, lighting, power supplies

4

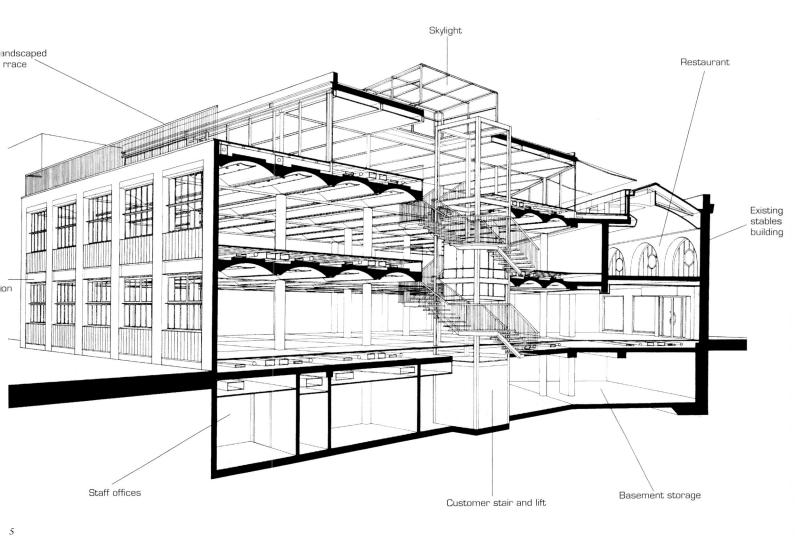

Skylight

Landscaped
terrace

Restaurant

Existing
stables
building

ion

Staff offices

Customer stair and lift

Basement storage

5

and air-conditioning. The cutouts to the concrete were combined with shadow gaps and bevelled rebates to ensure all edges remained crisp and sharp during the problematic release process from the mould.

Lighting pontoons were suspended under the concrete vaults, providing ideal provision for spot lighting of the goods below and subtle up-lighting to accentuate the flowing curves of the concrete above.

6

ATRIUM PERGOLA
SINGAPORE EXPO, CHANGI, REPUBLIC OF SINGAPORE
The Cox Group

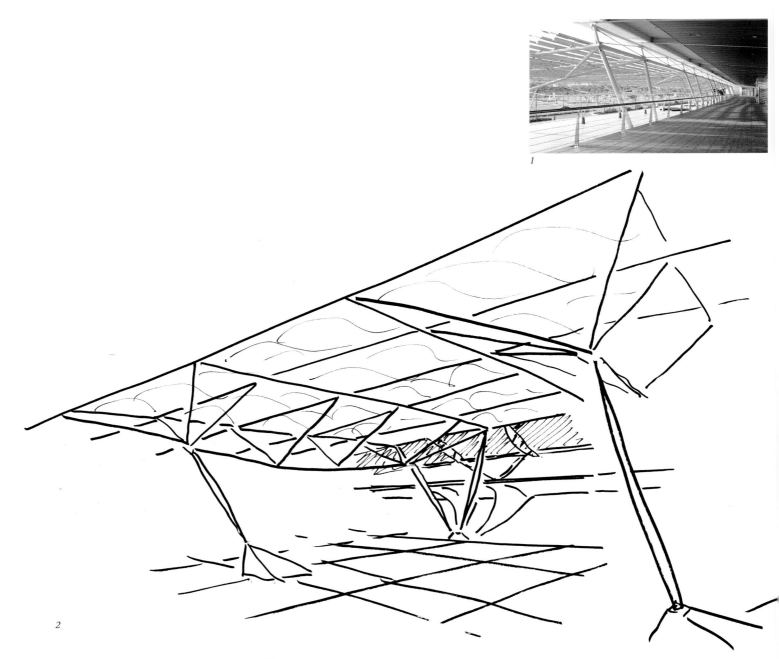

1

2

Singapore Expo is a 60,000-square-metre column-free exhibition centre. It is in fact a first stage, with a further 40,000 square metres designed for the final stage.

The selection of this design was partly based on the site, an awkward configuration rimmed by an elevated Mass Rapid Transit (MRT) system.

The roofs span 100 square metres and were designed to be fabricated on the exhibition floor and lifted in one operation over an eight-hour period.

They consist of three triangular section curved trusses with elevated bands for air extraction, this idea being interpreted from some of the traditional storage sheds along the Singapore waterfront. The structure is exposed both above and under the roof lining to articulate the forms, which are particularly dramatic at night.

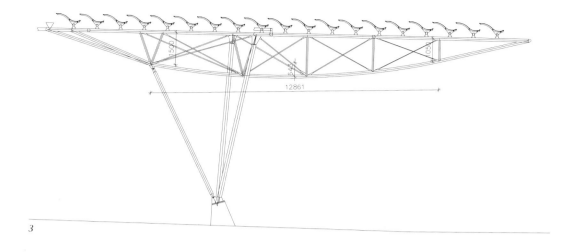

3

4

5

1   View into atrium
2   Atrium pergola concept sketch
3   Detail section of pergola
4   View of pergola at night
5   Pergola, frame and mesh detail
Photography: Graham Sands

ROOF TRUSS

SYDNEY SUPERDOME, HOMEBUSH BAY, NEW SOUTH WALES, AUSTRALIA
The Cox Group in association with Devine Deflon Yaegar

1

2

3

1 VIP foyer roof truss
2 Verandah colonnade column detail
3 Foyer and colonnade
4 Foyer roof truss
5 Truss node detail
6 Colonnade column detail
Photography: Patrick Bingham Hall

Sydney SuperDome was designed as a multi-use arena for the Sydney 2000 Olympic Games and as a major indoor sports and entertainment venue.

The SuperDome is conceived as a long horizontal and translucent building, scaled to unify with a lightweight verandah structure that wraps around two sides of the dome. Because the full scale of the SuperDome can only be appreciated from one location, a system of tall mast structures was developed around the stadium, like a coronet, which are visible from all surrounds. As a result, the total complex appears extremely delicate and permeable, in contrast to typically solid indoor sports centres. This appearance is accentuated by

a thin line of cantilevered and free-standing colonnade edges supported by fine tree-column structures. The cable-suspended truss roof system appears equally delicate yet spans 150 by 120 metres.

The arena is accessible from four levels – two public levels, a club level and a corporate box level – each serviced by food courts, bars, lounges and services. These provide significantly higher levels of public amenity than are conventionally offered; provide a focus on flexibility and choice and allows the implementation of new viewing technology.

4

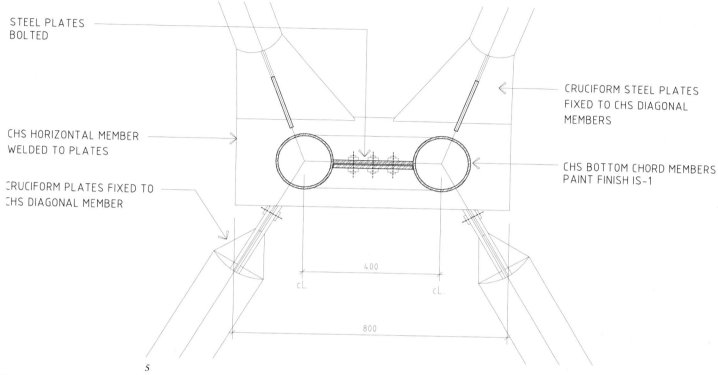

STEEL PLATES
BOLTED

CHS HORIZONTAL MEMBER
WELDED TO PLATES

CRUCIFORM PLATES FIXED TO
CHS DIAGONAL MEMBER

CRUCIFORM STEEL PLATES
FIXED TO CHS DIAGONAL
MEMBERS

CHS BOTTOM CHORD MEMBERS
PAINT FINISH IS-1

400

cL

cL.

800

5

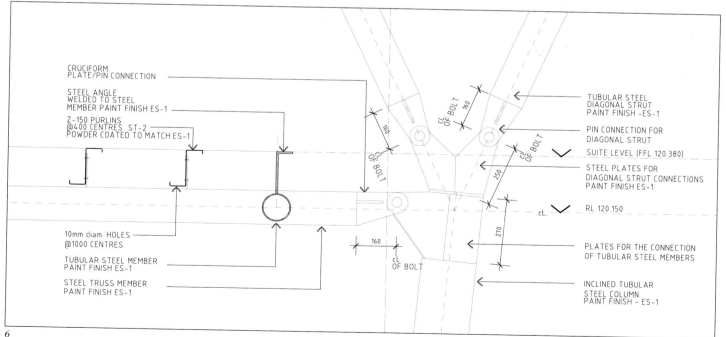

CRUCIFORM
PLATE/PIN CONNECTION

STEEL ANGLE
WELDED TO STEEL
MEMBER PAINT FINISH ES-1

Z-150 PURLINS
@400 CENTRES ST-2
POWDER COATED TO MATCH ES-1

10mm diam. HOLES
@1000 CENTRES

TUBULAR STEEL MEMBER
PAINT FINISH ES-1

STEEL TRUSS MEMBER
PAINT FINISH ES-1

cL
OF BOLT

160

cL
OF BOLT

160

cL
OF BOLT

250

cL
OF BOLT

270

160

cL
OF BOLT

TUBULAR STEEL
DIAGONAL STRUT
PAINT FINISH -ES-1

PIN CONNECTION FOR
DIAGONAL STRUT

SUITE LEVEL (FFL 120.380)

STEEL PLATES FOR
DIAGONAL STRUT CONNECTIONS
PAINT FINISH ES-1

cL. RL 120.150

PLATES FOR THE CONNECTION
OF TUBULAR STEEL MEMBERS

INCLINED TUBULAR
STEEL COLUMN
PAINT FINISH - ES-1

6

SCREEN
COLDSTREAM HILLS WINERY, COLDSTREAM, VICTORIA, AUSTRALIA
The Cox Group

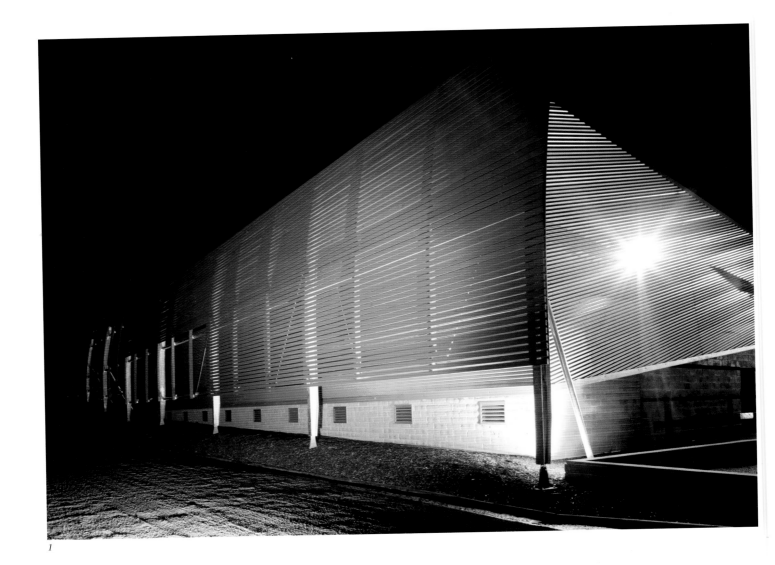

1

1   External night view
2   Timber screen section
Photography: Chris Ott

Coldstream Hills Winery in Victoria's Yarra Valley was developed in 1985 by James Halliday, and is now part of Southcorp Wines.

The project's aim was to upgrade site facilities to accommodate an increase in red wine production. These facilities include a new barrel hall for wine maturation, new road access, cellar door refurbishment and landscaping.

The new barrel store is sited on the southern headland of the vineyard amphitheatre, and is integrated with the landform to facilitate

temperature stability and at-grade access to the production facility. It comprises two elements: one with a stepped roof controlling ventilation, the other a slatted screen for diminishing heat loads.

The building is designed to convey the nature of its purpose through metaphoric association, and to reflect the distinctive image of the wine produced there.

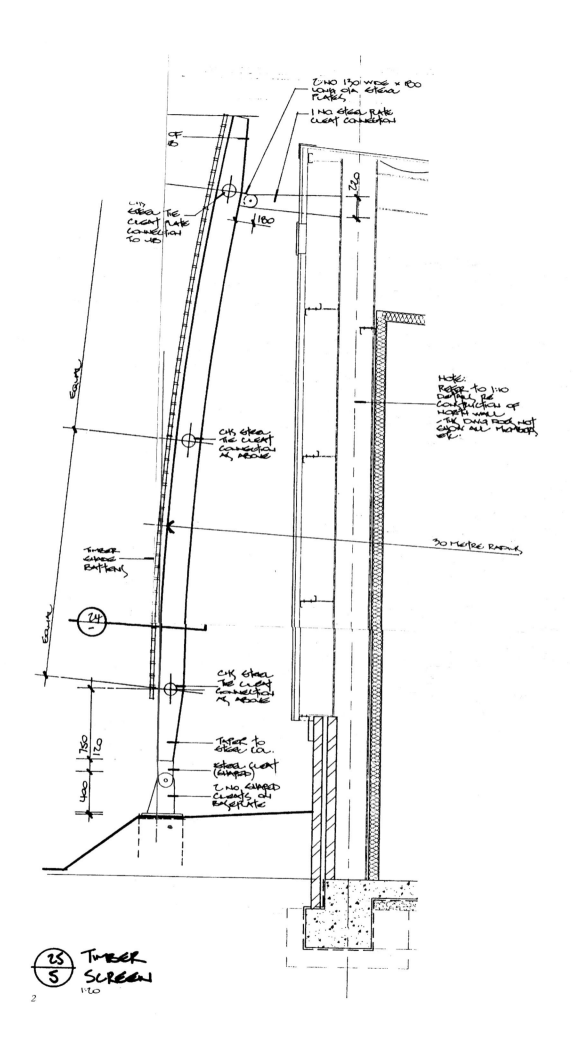

2 NO 130Ø WIDE x 180
LONG DIA STEEL
PLATES

1 NO STEEL PLATE
CLEAT CONNECTION

OF
1B

CHS STEEL TIE
CLEAT PLATE
CONNECTION
TO 1B

180

720

CHS STEEL
TIE CLEAT
CONNECTION
AS ABOVE

NOTE:
REFER TO 1:10
DETAIL RE
CONSTRUCTION OF
NORTH WALL
THE DWG DOES NOT
SHOW ALL MEMBERS
ETC.

30 METRE RADIUS

TIMBER
SHAPED
BATTENS

24
—

CHS STEEL
TIE CLEAT
CONNECTION
AS ABOVE

TAPER TO
STEEL CO.

STEEL CLEAT
(SHAPED)

2 NO SHAPED
CLEATS ON
BASEPLATE

750 | 120

400

25
5

TIMBER
SCREEN

1:20

2

ORNAMENTAL RAIL AND COLUMN

RITZ-CARLTON RESORT, SHARM EL SHIEKH, EGYPT
DiLeonardo International, Inc.

1

The Ritz-Carlton, Sharm El Sheikh, is a 307-room luxury hotel overlooking the environmentally protected waters of the Red Sea.

While the site plan reinforces the natural lay of the land, the built environment works to intensify the colours, forms and history of the location. The locally sourced material selected for the project is crucial to the interior experience.

The reflective nature of the lobby flooring combined with running water and sparkling gold accents link the experience to the sea. Oversized portals mark transitions to new environments.

Each guestroom block resonates with similar design principles; water views are unobstructed from the stepped terraces, and sunshades and planting bring a level of intimacy to each guestroom, while reinforcing the indoor/outdoor experience.

The ornamental rail detailing and column details are used on both the interior and exterior of the building. These were designed to reflect Pharaonic motifs found throughout the region. Simple detailing solutions were employed to match local construction methods – this includes stone detailing and cast plasterwork.

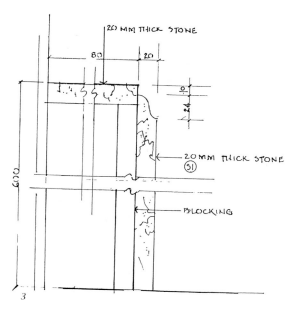

20 MM THICK STONE

80   20

24

600

20 MM THICK STONE
(S1)

BLOCKING

3

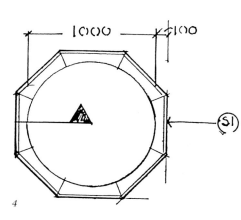

1000   100

(S1)   SEGMENTED POLISHED
STONE BASE

4

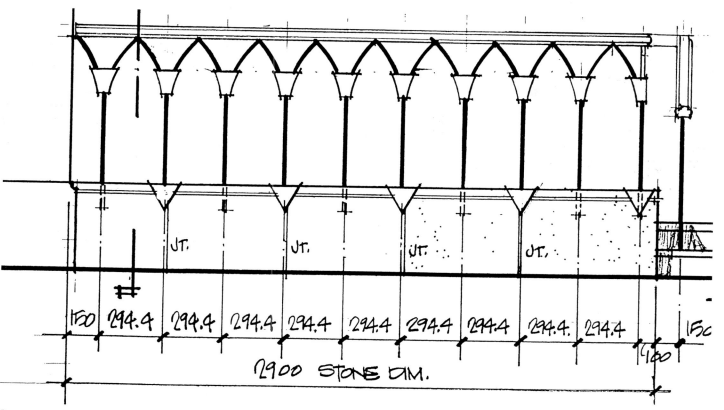

JT.   JT.   JT.   JT.

150 | 294.4 | 294.4 | 294.4 | 294.4 | 294.4 | 294.4 | 294.4 | 294.4 | 294.4 | 150

100

2900 STONE DIM.

5

PARK AND PLAYGROUND

KAINAN WANPAKU PARK, KAINAN, JAPAN
Mitsuru Senda + Environment Design Institute

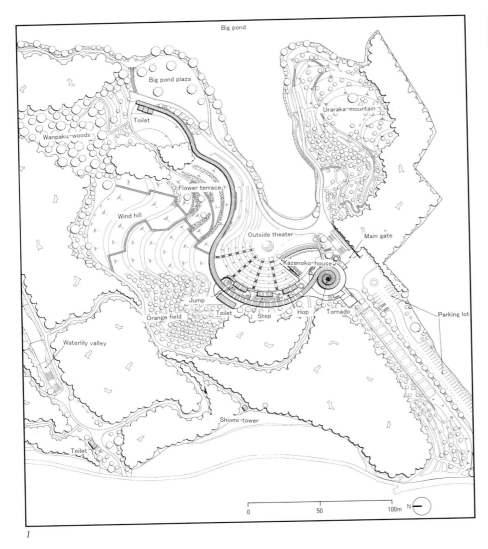

Big pond

Big pond plaza

Toilet

Wanpaku-woods

Uraraka-mountain

Flower terrace

Wind hill

Outside theater

Main gate

Kazenoko-house

Jump

Orange field   Toilet   Step   Hop   Tornado

Parking lot

Waterlily valley

Shiomi-tower

Toilet

0   50   100m   N

1

2

3

4

In the years between primary school and high school children can exhibit various social problems which may be driven by a lack of rich play experience. Mitsuru Senda has long studied the development of the play environment, especially for primary school children, and has given many warnings about Japanese children's lack of play experience and possible consequences for the future of Japan.

Children's issues are generally discussed by adults, with the thought that children can make their own play spaces. However, parents are now realising that children need their own space and a free and easy environment for play. Consequently, they are searching for well-designed play areas which gives local governments an incentive to construct parks for children to play.

Kainan Wanpaku Park is a place of natural beauty with a pond and various wooded areas. The park has been designed with various play areas for children of all ages. One such play area designed for younger children is called *Hop Step & Jump*. The play equipment is at the start of a path of steps that leads from the equipment to group play areas and finally to the woods.

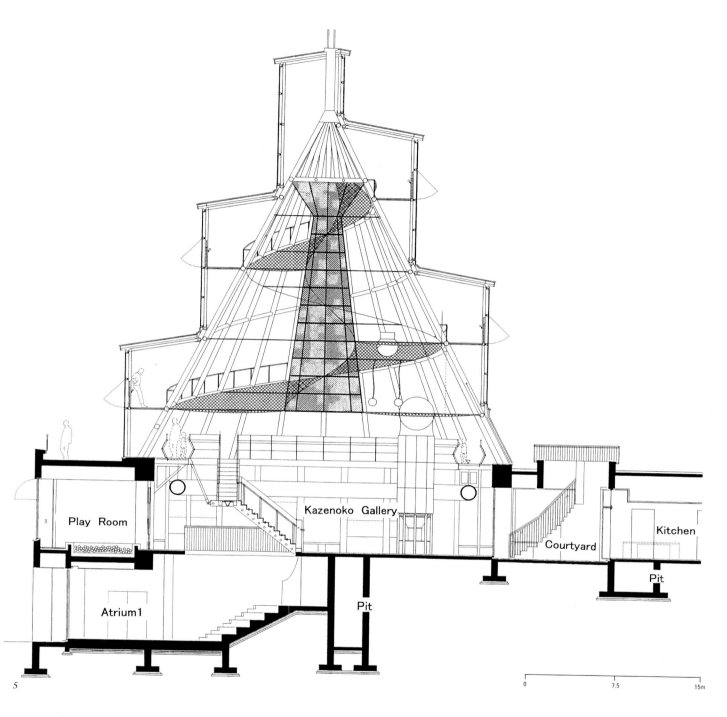

Play Room

Kazenoko Gallery

Kitchen

Courtyard

Pit

Atrium1

Pit

| 0 | 7.5 | 15m |

5

6

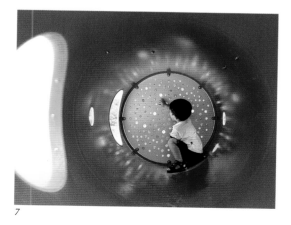

7

1   Site plan
2   Kazenoko building from north
3   Overall view from eastern pond
4   Hop, Step & Jump
5   Section of playroom
6   Looking up spiral net into tornado
7   Marbles on 'Step' tube
Photography: Mitsumasa Fujitsuka

CLERESTORIES

CLARK COUNTY GOVERNMENT CENTER, LAS VEGAS, NEVADA, USA
Fentress Bradburn Architects

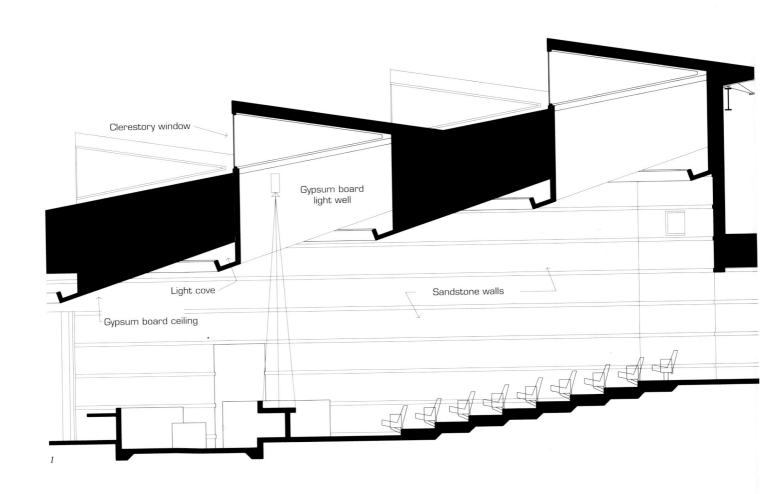

Clerestory window

Gypsum board
light well

Light cove

Sandstone walls

Gypsum board ceiling

1

With their triangular shape, the clerestories on the roof of the Commissioners Chamber of the Clark County Government Center render the sharpness of cactus spines. The design was inspired by imagery of the surrounding Las Vegas desert.

On the outside of the building where they protrude, the phalanx of shapes – triangular both vertically and horizontally – creates a texture in contrast to the rest of the building.

On the inside, the clerestories flood the space with light during the day. A series of hidden light coves illuminate the clerestories at night, so that the chamber continues to be lit from above. These also help organise the space for visitors, as the points of the clerestories are directed towards the council seats at the front of the chamber.

Originally, the roof of the Commissioners Chamber was to be clad in ceramic tile referencing the texture of the prickly pear cactus. When this was deemed too ostentatious by the client, the materials were modified to a single-ply bitumen membrane with a custom-coloured, coil-coated aluminium exterior finish.

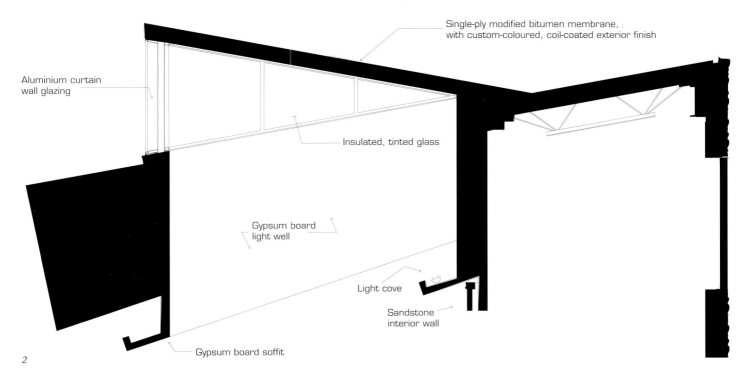

Single-ply modified bitumen membrane, with custom-coloured, coil-coated exterior finish

Aluminium curtain wall glazing

Insulated, tinted glass

Gypsum board light well

Light cove

Sandstone interior wall

Gypsum board soffit

2

3

4

1   Commissioners Chamber section
2   Clerestory section
3   Clerestories in Commissioners Chamber reference prickly pear cactus
4   Clerestories cut Commissioners Chambers ceiling with sharp shapes
Photography: Nick Merrick, Hedrich Blessing

SCULPTURAL LAMP

CLARK COUNTY GOVERNMENT CENTER, LAS VEGAS, NEVADA, USA
Fentress Bradburn Architects

1

2

3

Imagery of the desert surrounding Las Vegas, from canyons and mountains to desert flowers and cactus, guided the design of this building. The tough vines of desert plants are depicted in the sculptural lamps that stand in the lobby of the building's rotunda as well as in its pyramidal community space.

The architects were originally inspired by a towering saguaro cactus from which much of the flesh had eroded. Braided steel bars have been bent to form the skeleton shape.

In keeping with other materials in the complex, the base of the lamp was crafted from sandstone. The steel pyramid-shaped luminaire at the top not only represents a desert bloom but is also an inverted replica of the complex's pyramid-shaped employee cafeteria. The luminaires are closed at the top with sheet metal that is punctuated with variously shaped holes to allow light to emerge, as if through the crevices between rocks. An acrylic lens behind the metal serves to diffuse the light source.

Steel Pyramid
Luminaire

1 View between lamps to skylight
2 Pyramid inspired by desert mountain imagery
3 Slotted skylights inside employee cafeteria give an
   exhilarating experience of sky; lamps use the pyramid
   in inverted form
4 Lamps emulate desert blooms and tough vines
5 Elevation of sculptural lamp
Photography: Timothy Hursley (1&2), Nick Merrick,
Hedrick Blessing (3&4)

(4) ³⁄₄" Twisted
steel bar

4

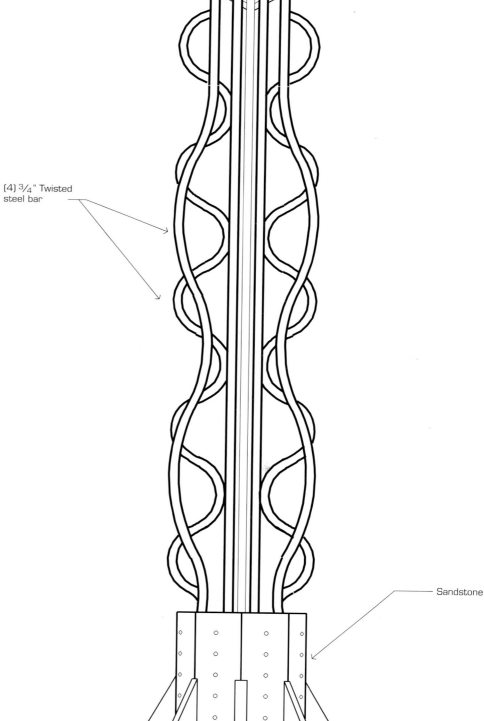

Sandstone

Steel Support
Fins

5

SKYLIGHT SCREEN
CLARK COUNTY GOVERNMENT CENTER, LAS VEGAS, NEVADA, USA
Fentress Bradburn Architects

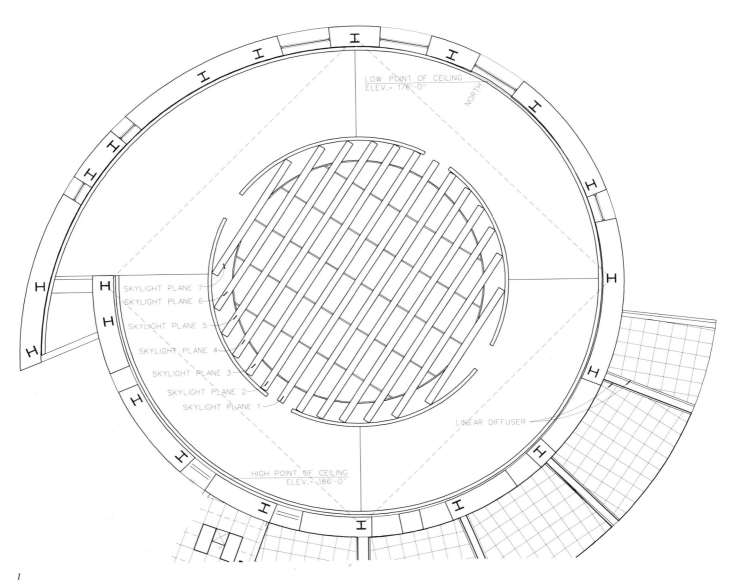

LOW POINT OF CEILING
ELEV.= 176'-0"

NORTH

SKYLIGHT PLANE 7
SKYLIGHT PLANE 6
SKYLIGHT PLANE 5
SKYLIGHT PLANE 4
SKYLIGHT PLANE 3
SKYLIGHT PLANE 2
SKYLIGHT PLANE 1

LINEAR DIFFUSER

HIGH POINT OF CEILING
ELEV.= 186'-0"

1

2

Design of the Clark County Government Center was guided by the desert imagery surrounding Las Vegas. The rotunda of the building was made in a solid shape reminiscent of the region's 'pot-hole' canyons that offer respite from the light and heat of the desert.

The architects wanted to fill the space with light but minimize solar gain, so they topped the rotunda with a skylight, but screened the sunlight through a sculptural shape. The idea was to simulate the experience of seeing light through crevices in desert rock formations. The screen changes the light in the space as the day progresses. Direct light penetrates all the way to the rotunda floor at noon, but light is only reflected into the space by the sculptural screen for most of the remainder of the day.

The screen is made of 13 parallel slabs in an undulating form that hangs down into the space. Hung on a steel frame, these slabs are created out of steel studs and gypsum board with an acrylic coating finish to simulate the look of sandstone.

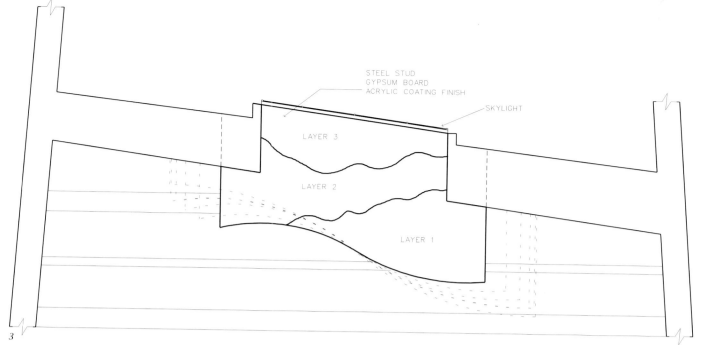

STEEL STUD
GYPSUM BOARD
ACRYLIC COATING FINISH

SKYLIGHT

LAYER 3

LAYER 2

LAYER 1

3

4

5

The slabs differ in length as they occupy the circular shape of the skylight and the wave shape of each is slightly different from the others. In addition, three layers of drywall cut in various shapes were applied to each slab to reference the changing textures of rough canyon walls.

1 Reflected ceiling plan of entry lobby
2 Triangular stairway cuts sharp form into lobby
3 Elevation of skylight plane
4 Detail of screen sculpture at lobby ceiling
5 Rotunda ceiling sculpture screens sun coming through skylight

Photography: Nick Merricks, Hedrich Blessing (1,4), Timothy Hursley (5)

CEILING

THE CONDÉ NAST BUILDING @ FOUR TIMES SQUARE, NEW YORK, NEW YORK, USA
Fox & Fowle Architects

1

The Condé Nast Building @ Four Times Square, a 48-storey office tower, is the centrepiece of the master plan prepared by the 42nd Street Development Corporation, a public/private consortium created to promote the redevelopment of the heart of Manhattan.

The building straddles several great urban spaces with diverse identities, including Times Square's unfettered commercialism, Bryant Park's urbanity and the midtown business district's composure. Its design embraces the essence of Times Square while meeting the needs of corporate tenants – a successful marriage of pop culture and corporate standards.

Aluminum leaf curves down parabolically and forms the scalloped ceiling of the lobby. Visible from the exterior through glass curtain wall, the elegant, yet playful form of the ceiling connects the building's two main entrances at 42nd and 43rd Streets.

This project announces a major statement for environmental responsibility. It is the first project of its size in the United States to set new standards for energy conservation, indoor environmental quality, recycling systems and the use of sustainable materials.

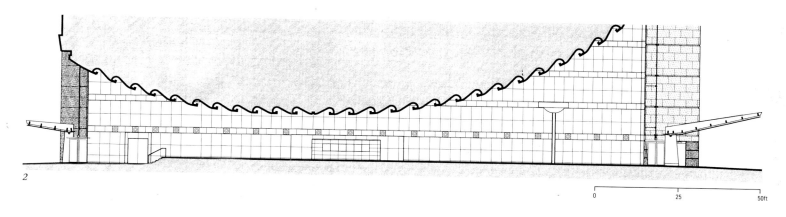

2

0　　　　　25　　　　　50ft

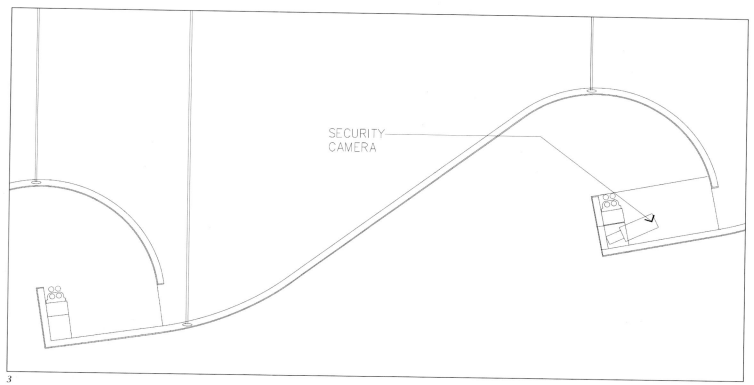

SECURITY
CAMERA

3

4

1&4　Interior of lobby showing ceiling
2　Section of lobby
3　Detail of ceiling
*Photography: Andrew Gordon. Drawings:
courtesy of Fox & Fowle Architects*

CANOPY
DEPARTMENT OF VETERANS AFFAIRS MEDICAL CENTER, ANN ARBOR, MICHIGAN, USA
HarleyEllis

1

2

3

The Department of Veterans Affairs Medical Campus located in Ann Arbor, Michigan, has been serving patients since 1949 through an existing 400-bed main hospital and a 160-bed nursing care facility. Constructed in the early 1950s, when the centre was treating less than 30 patients, the facility provides primary and specialty healthcare to more than 21,000 veterans in southern Michigan and northwestern Ohio.

Serving as the campus showpiece, the 31,586-square-metre clinical addition boasts strong architectural elements framed by a graceful curving entry canopy. Situated as the main campus entrance, the eight-storey building contains fully accessible interstitial space between each floor, simplifying future systems modifications while minimising patient interference.

The building is clad in red brick with limestone trim, complementing the existing campus structure. This palette blends with crisply detailed curtainwalls of green glass and white porcelain metal panels forming a contemporary complement distinctive in its own right.

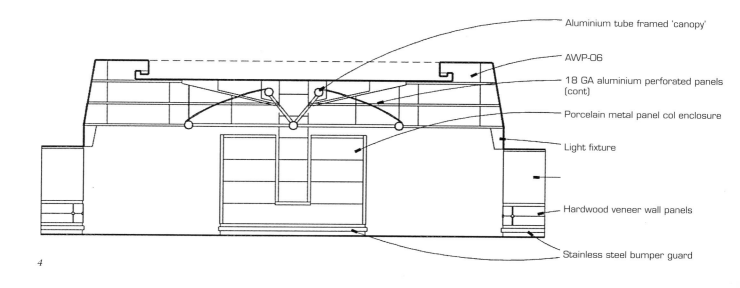

Aluminium tube framed 'canopy'

AWP-06

18 GA aluminium perforated panels
(cont)

Porcelain metal panel col enclosure

Light fixture

Hardwood veneer wall panels

Stainless steel bumper guard

4

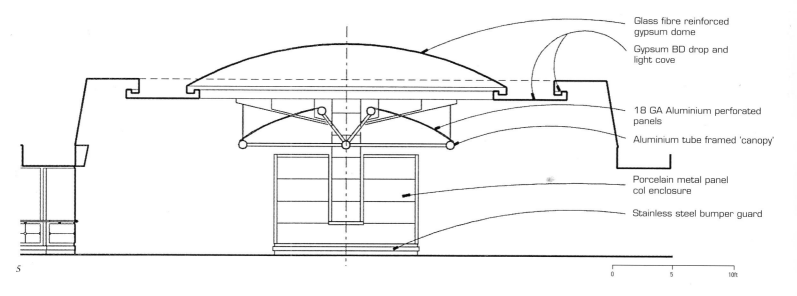

Glass fibre reinforced
gypsum dome

Gypsum BD drop and
light cove

18 GA Aluminium perforated
panels

Aluminium tube framed 'canopy'

Porcelain metal panel
col enclosure

Stainless steel bumper guard

5

0   5   10ft

The interior environment is progressive;
aesthetically appealing; appropriate to patients,
visitors and staff; and reflective of the technology
contained within.

1,2&3 *Reception waiting area showing*
       canopy and dome
  4&5 *Detail of lighting canopy and dome*
       in reception waiting area
Photography: Hedrich Blessing courtesy of
HarleyEllis

STAIRS
CUBE GALLERY, MANCHESTER, UK
Hodder Associates

1

2

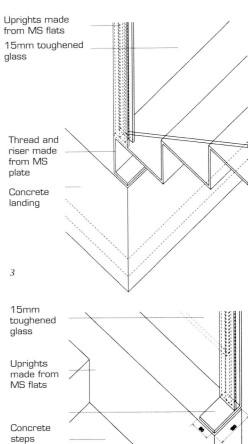

Uprights made from MS flats

15mm toughened glass

Thread and riser made from MS plate

Concrete landing

3

15mm toughened glass

Uprights made from MS flats

Concrete steps and landing

4

CUBE is essentially a centre for architecture, part of a network being established throughout the United Kingdom. It represents an important public forum for the display and debate of architecture.

Located in a Grade II listed former cotton warehouse, the refurbishment and conversion of the two floors that make up the gallery seeks to add a further contemporary layer to the historic framework.

The entrance to the two ground floor galleries and the RIBA Bookshop is via a new foyer, which presents an anonymous front to both CUBE and the offices within the remainder of the building.

The galleries are quite simple, with a subtle interplay of new screens and diffuse side glazing set against the conserved enclosure. Serviced nodes articulate the spaces and a new oak floor gives coherence to the whole.

Two new staircases of folded steel descend to the basement gallery and lecture room. The treatment of these spaces is very similar to the ground floor with natural light permeating from rooflights above.

1 Angle section handraid made from MS flats
2 12.5mm plasterboard on SW stud frame
3 Expamet shadow bead
4 15mm toughened glass
5 Top edge of glass

6 80x10mm toughened MS upriht
7 12.5mm plasterboard on SW stud frame
8 Bottom edge of glass
9 Stair made from 8mm MS plate
10 Expamet stop bead
11 12.5mm plasterboard

12 30x30mm MS upright
13 80x10mm MS upright screwed to MS block
14 15mm toughened glass
15 80x10mm MS upright welded to MS tread

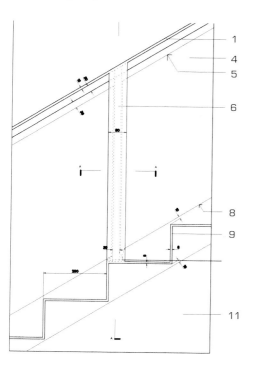

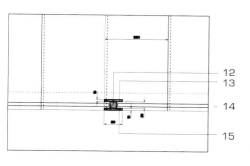

5

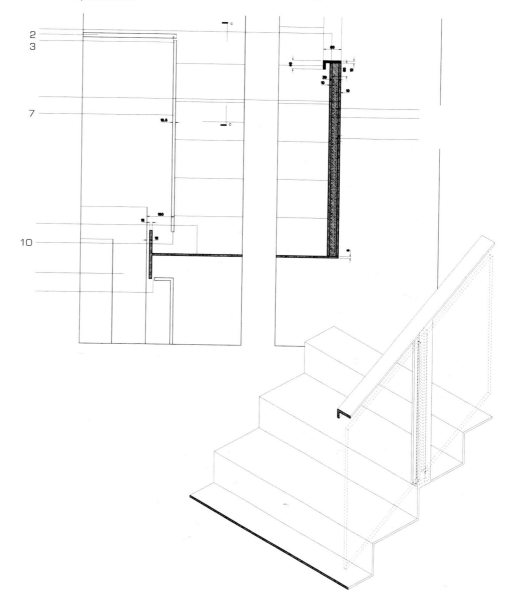

Photography: Peter Cook

6

GLAZED BRIDGE

CATHARIJNECONVENT, UTRECHT, THE NETHERLANDS
Hubert-Jan Henket architecten bna

1

1 *Exterior glass bridge*
2 *Section*
3 *Detail*

The Utrecht City Council redeveloped the Lange Nieuwtraat as part of its Museum Quarter project.

The project required moving the entrance of Catharijneconvent from the other side of the complex. It also required the enabling of the public to cross the complex to the Nieywegracht without entering the museum. Therefore, two separate routes were required, largely for security reasons, which cross each other. The only way to do this was with separate levels.

The collection is housed in different buildings, making orientation though the complex difficult for visitors, but this has been made more user-friendly with the completion of a glazed bridge.

The bridge changes their orientation once they have purchased tickets and entered the cloister via the underground tunnel. It has also provided a cover over the walkway.

A new staircase and lift was also included in the redevelopment, providing a view of the total vertical building construction of the cloister, and a view of the public route; this assists museum visitors to identify the new entrance. The new staircase was made using wood recycled from the old staircase.

The dividing walls have been made more transparent. An enormous vertical window has been incorporated into the existing staircase to

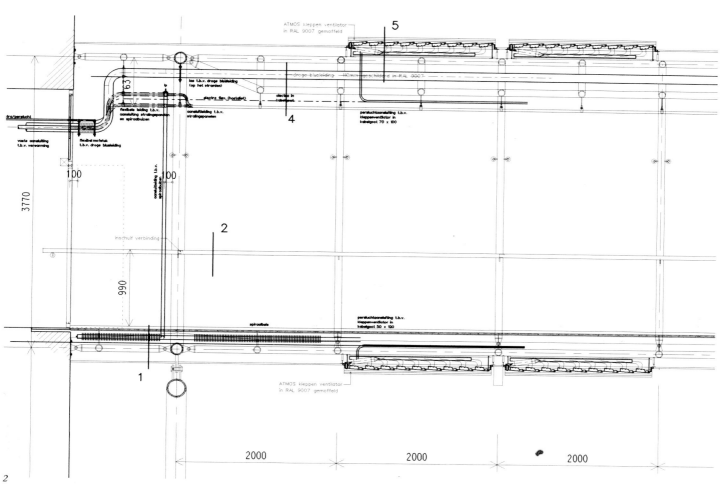

ATMOS kleppen ventilator
in RAL 9007 gemoffeld

5

droge blusleiding 110mm geschilderd in RAL 9007

lus t.b.v. droge blusleiding
(op het stramien)

electra flex (hootlatlat)

electra in
kabelgoot

persluchtaansluiting t.b.v.
kleppenventilator in
kabelgoot 70 x 100

63

flexibele leiding t.b.v.
aansluiting stralingspanelen
en spiraalbuizen

aansluitleiding t.b.v.
stralingspanelen

4

vaste aansluiting
t.b.v. verwarming

flexibel metstuk
t.b.v. droge blusleiding

100   100

3770

aansluitleiding t.b.v.
spiraalbuizen

2

inschuif verbinding

990

persluchtaansluiting t.b.v.
kleppenventilator in
kabelgoot 50 x 120

spiraalbuis

1

ATMOS kleppen ventilator
in RAL 9007 gemoffeld

2000   2000   2000

2

create extra daylight and to connect some of the elevated exhibition rooms with the rest of the complex. This window will be used to exhibit the museum's beautiful permanent stained glass collection.

The redevelopment also includes a refit of the heating, ventilation and electrical installations.

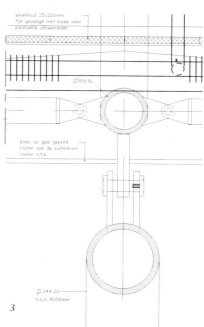

eikenhout 25x200mm
fijn gezaagd met losse veer
plaatselijk uitneembaar

Ø159.16

baan op glas geprint
raster aan de buitenkant
raster n.t.b.

Ø 244.20
h.o.h. 8000mm

3

4   Section
5   Interior glass bridge
6   Detail of heating system
7   Beneath glazed bridge
8   Section through glazed bridge
Photography: architectuurfotografie Sybolt
Voeten/Michel Kievits

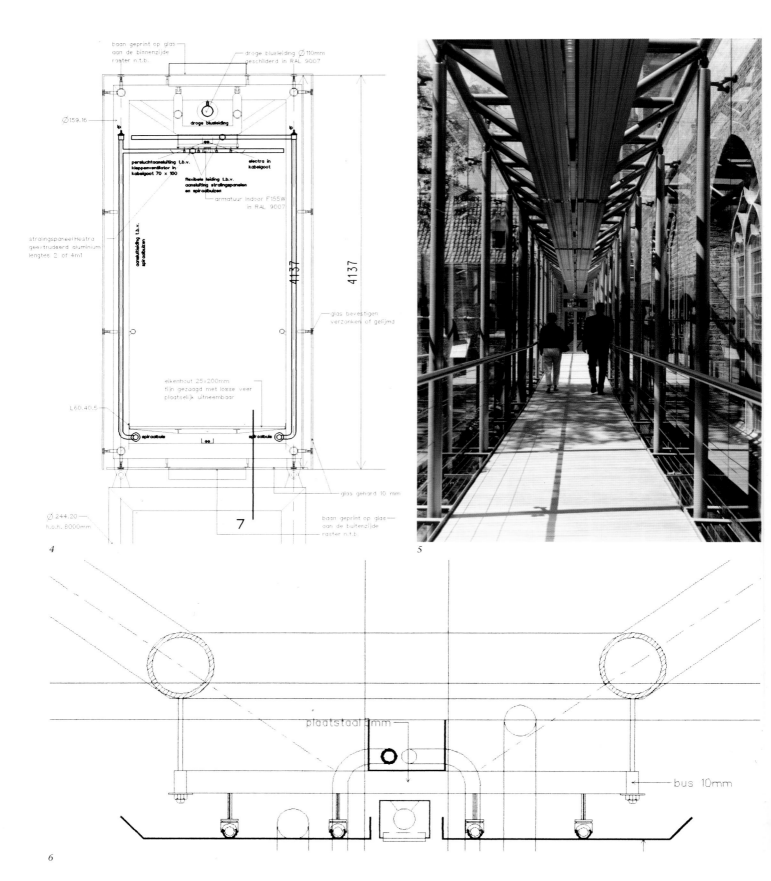

4

5

6

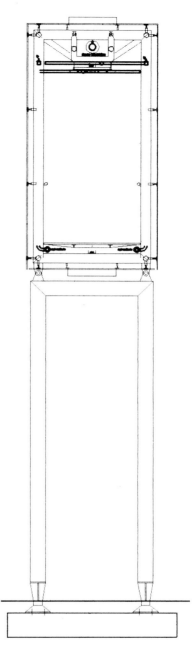

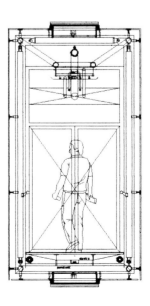

7

8

LOUVRES AND WALL

GRANT HOUSE, SURRY HILLS, NSW, AUSTRALIA
Jahn Associates Architects

1

2

1   View from courtyard across pond to
    entrance; Alucobond anodised louvres
    create privacy screen for bedrooms
2   The juxtaposition of natural and man-
    made materials reflects the different
    functions of the spaces
3   Louvre section

This city house for client Stephen Grant has been
built within the shell of an old timber-yard in the
back streets of inner-city Sydney. The new
enclosure is a folded plane of successive skins of
brick, eco-plywood and corrugated metal sheeting.
The layering of materials and the folded surface
brings a new dimension to the street through the
simplicity of volume.

Entirely contained within the original brick walls,
the new building is stacked to the south, enabling
a ground-level courtyard to emerge. This courtyard
is embraced, overlooked, intersected, screened and
infused by the fabric of the building; the interior as

a whole engaging in a play of spatial relationships
and materials that is rarely afforded by the
predominantly 19th century terrace houses or 20th
century strata-titled apartment buildings of
Sydney. Sydney provides few opportunities for an
integrated spatial environment for negative and
positive space but they require the exploration
evident in the Grant House.

Jahn Associates Architects has won two awards for
this project, including the Robin Boyd Award for
National Residential Design, and a NSW Chapter
Merit Award from the Royal Australian Institute of
Architects.

A   Louvre channel
B   Injection moulded polypropylene clips
      natural anodised aluminium finish
C   Reinforced concrete blade wall,
      battens and concrete ties of
      formwork to detail
D   Pivot bearing secured to the
      activating bars housed within the
      channel – operating mechanism
      grouped
E   Hexagonal shaped louvres
F   S/S domed flat head screws, 2 per
      connection
G   Slip joint
H   Paving on pads to courtyard

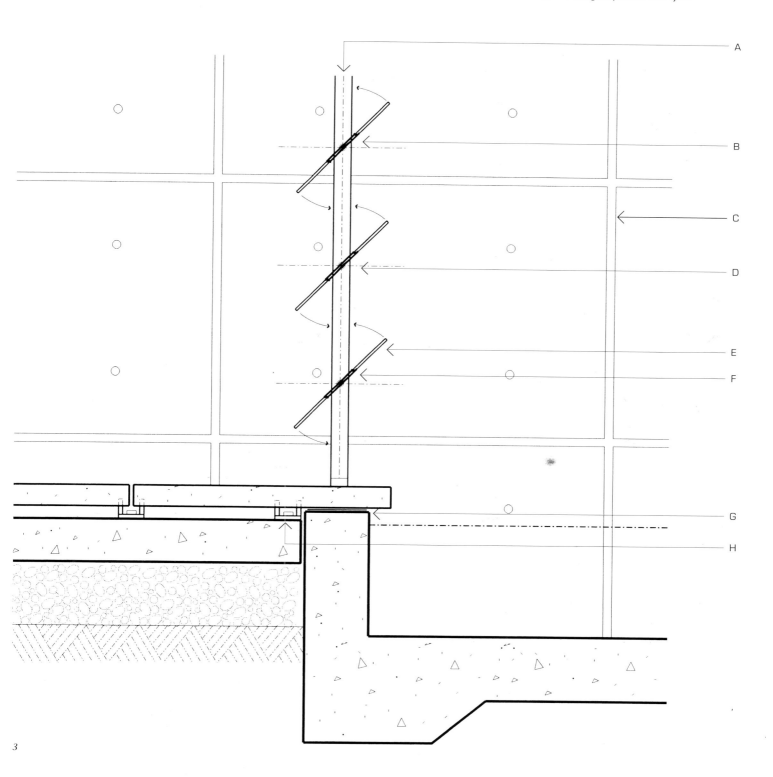

3

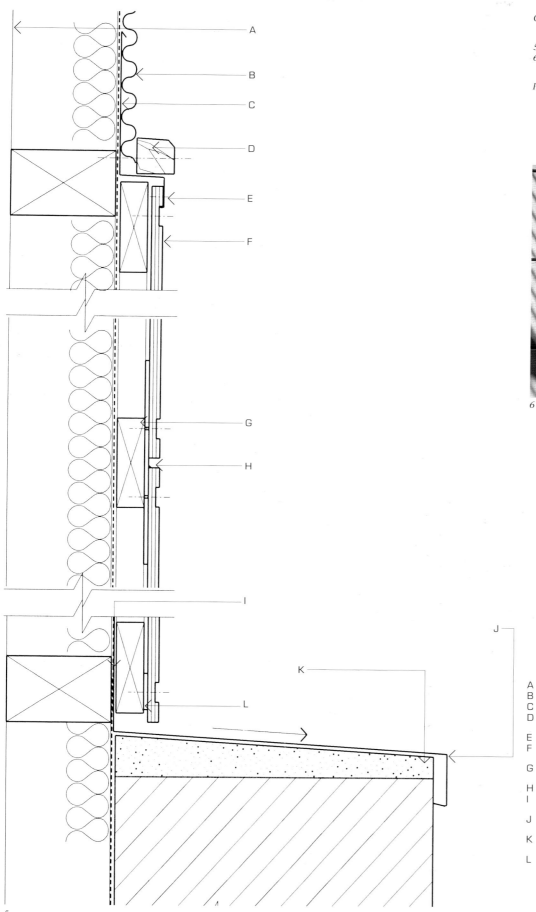

Opposite
  New entry of steel and needled concrete
  was inserted into original brick walls
5 *Wall section*
6 *Timber battens and concrete ties were used*
  to create the grid-like detailing of the
  concrete blade wall
Photography: Brett Boardman

6

A   Plasterboard
B   Colorbond custom-orb cladding
C   Continuous sarking
D   Profiled hardwood timber capping
    continuous around building perimeter
E   Powder coated metal flashing
F   Direct fix ecoply to dressed timber
    battens and spacers
G   Dressed ex 100x38 backing
    battens
H   3mm epoxy fillet
I   Silicon seal between sarking and
    DPC
J   Aluminium flashing, powder coated
    finish
K   Rendered capping to existing brick
    wall
L   Hardipanel backing strip

5

SLOPED GLAZING SYSTEM
SAILS PAVILION, SAN DIEGO CONVENTION CENTER, SAN DIEGO, CALIFORNIA, USA
Joseph Wong Design Associates

1

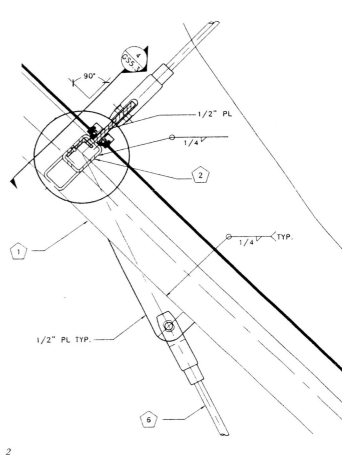

2

1 Interior view
2 Detail of cable support connections
3 Section through sloped glazing

The San Diego Convention Center has embarked on significant improvements to enhance the multifunctionality of the Sails Pavilion that encloses the 8,360-square-metre, column-free outdoor exhibit area. The deck space has a roof-tent structure, which is symbolic of sails on the bay. It was originally open on all sides.

Enhancements to the enclosure include the addition of industry-standard trade show floor amenities, lighting, air-conditioning, a fire suppression system, a light-transmitting wall and roof-infill system.

The preservation of the original open-air design and the maintenance of the maximum exposure to natural light was required in the design criteria.

The existing fabric tent roof typically has vaulted and curved opening configurations dictated by the outline and sloping of the fabric and cable supports. The east-side opening has a full-height and full-width laminated glass enclosure with light truss and cable supports. Fabric pillow top infill has been used. The west side opening has been enclosed with a solid, sound-attenuated wall with finishes matching the existing plaster walls.

The enclosure method for the typical north and south vaulted bay openings was challenging. It addresses the existing roof tent drainage and complies with the aesthetic, natural light, and structural design requirements. The new bay enclosure has adequate integrity to carry its weight

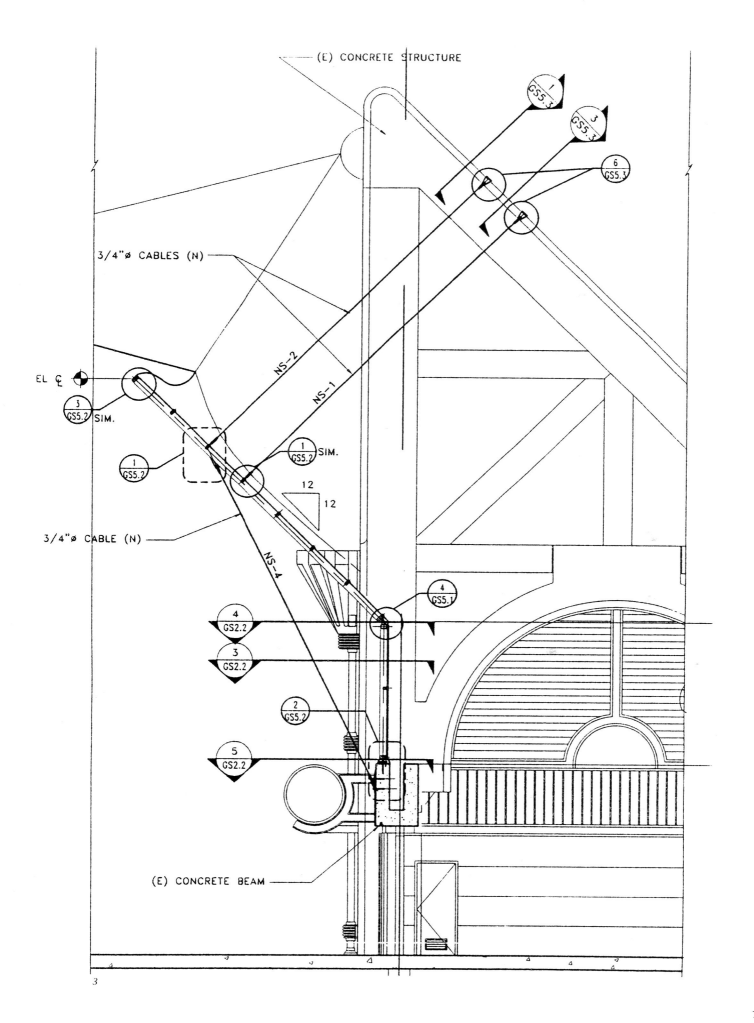

(E) CONCRETE STRUCTURE

3/4"ø CABLES (N)

3/4"ø CABLE (N)

(E) CONCRETE BEAM

EL ℄

NS-2

NS-1

NS-4

12

12

SIM.

SIM.

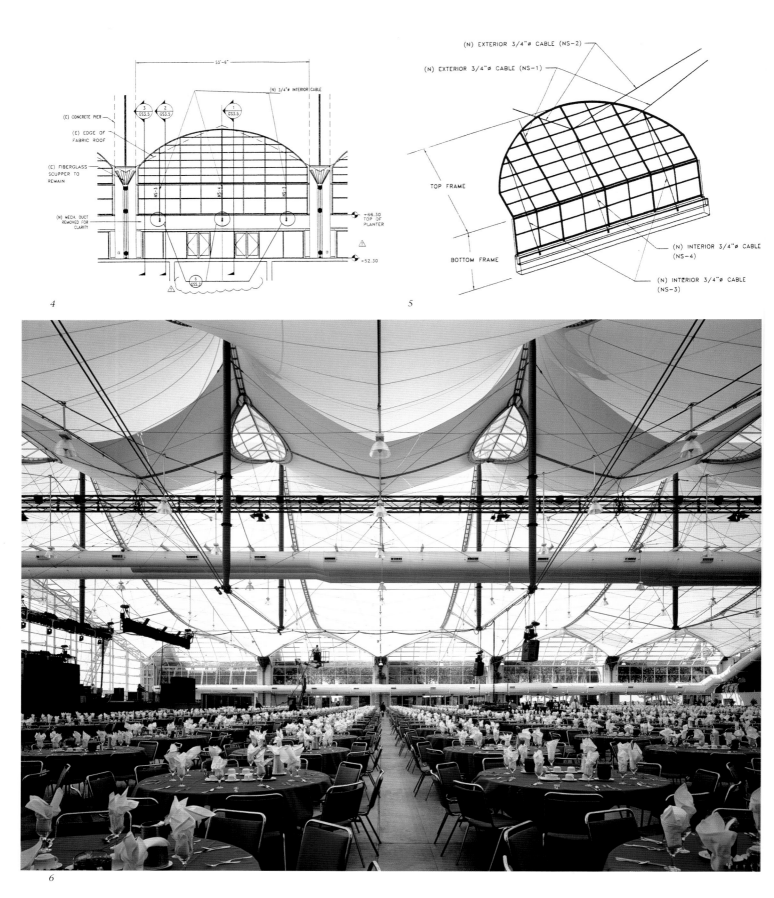

Labels in figure 4 (left diagram):
- 55'-6"
- (N) 3/4"ø INTERIOR CABLE
- (E) CONCRETE PIER
- (E) EDGE OF FABRIC ROOF
- (E) FIBERGLASS SCUPPER TO REMAIN
- (N) MECH. DUCT REMOVED FOR CLARITY
- +66.30 TOP OF PLANTER
- +52.30
- 3 GS3.5
- 2 GS3.5
- 1 GS3.5
- NS-3
- NS-1
- NS-1
- 5 GS5.2

Labels in figure 5 (right diagram):
- (N) EXTERIOR 3/4"ø CABLE (NS-2)
- (N) EXTERIOR 3/4"ø CABLE (NS-1)
- TOP FRAME
- BOTTOM FRAME
- (N) INTERIOR 3/4"ø CABLE (NS-4)
- (N) INTERIOR 3/4"ø CABLE (NS-3)

4

5

6

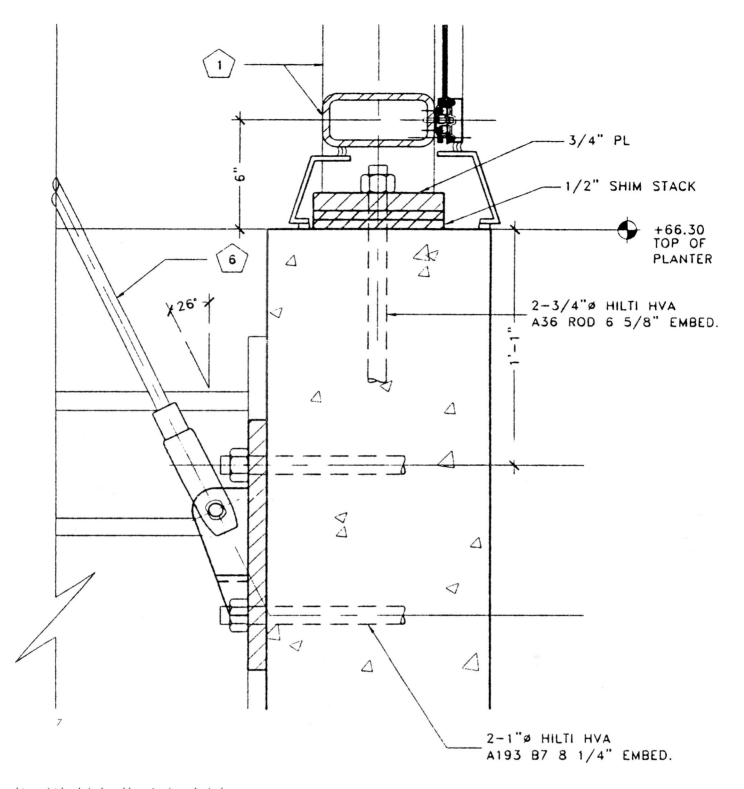

1

3/4" PL

1/2" SHIM STACK

6"

⊕ +66.30
TOP OF
PLANTER

6

26°

2-3/4"ø HILTI HVA
A36 ROD 6 5/8" EMBED.

1'-1"

7

2-1"ø HILTI HVA
A193 B7 8 1/4" EMBED.

and to resist loads induced by seismic and wind forces and the existing roof movements and loads.

The lightweight, sloped glazing system comprised of laminated glass and steel framework was selected following design, engineering, cost comparisons and explorations. This system follows the contour of the existing roof fabric and utilises fabric infills between the system and the existing tent edges. Structural cabling has been used extensively to support all the imposed loads and for stability. The result is a transparent bay enclosure in harmony with, and preserving the open-sail design.

4 Interior elevation of typical bay
5 Exterior isometric view of typical bay
6 Interior view
7 Detail of cable support and glazing system at base

Photography: Brady Architectural Photography

DOME
IZUMO DOME, IZUMO, JAPAN
Kajima Design

1

This design was selected above other entries for the Izumo City local government's all-weather multipurpose sporting stadium.

The open-air-style indoor environment afforded by the single-sheet, membranous domed roof; visual continuity with the outdoors; provision of utilities to counteract heavy snowfall; flexible level design; movable stand; integration of a fly system into the framework; timber and steel hybrid construction; and the overall layout to enable planning and management for every kind of sporting.

The transmission of natural light into the dome has been aided by the composition of the roof as a single layer of membrane, using as few members as possible to make the indoor space bright and pleasant. To make the dome appear to integrate with the park and to strengthen the feeling of continuity of inside and outside, an effect of total openness was achieved by lifting the base of the dome on 36 pillars and introducing large, polycarbonate jalousies for the 6-metre-high wall on all sides.

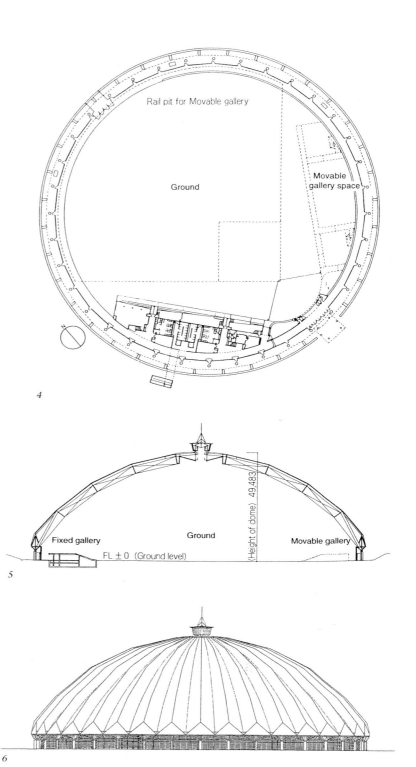

4

2

3

5

6

For ease of maintenance, special apparatus for the control and production of the interior environment have been concentrated in the central ring. This apparatus has been integrated with the frame. The diameter of the central ring is 22 metres to fit the lighting equipment, and the monitor for ventilation was installed in the 5-metre-high ring in the middle.

1 Aerial view
2 Central ring above ground
3 General view
4 First floor plan
5 Section
6 Elevation

7 Upward view of hybrid structural system
8 Large size louvred door
9 Detailed section of upper part and lower part of dome
Photography: Nishinihon Shabo

7

8

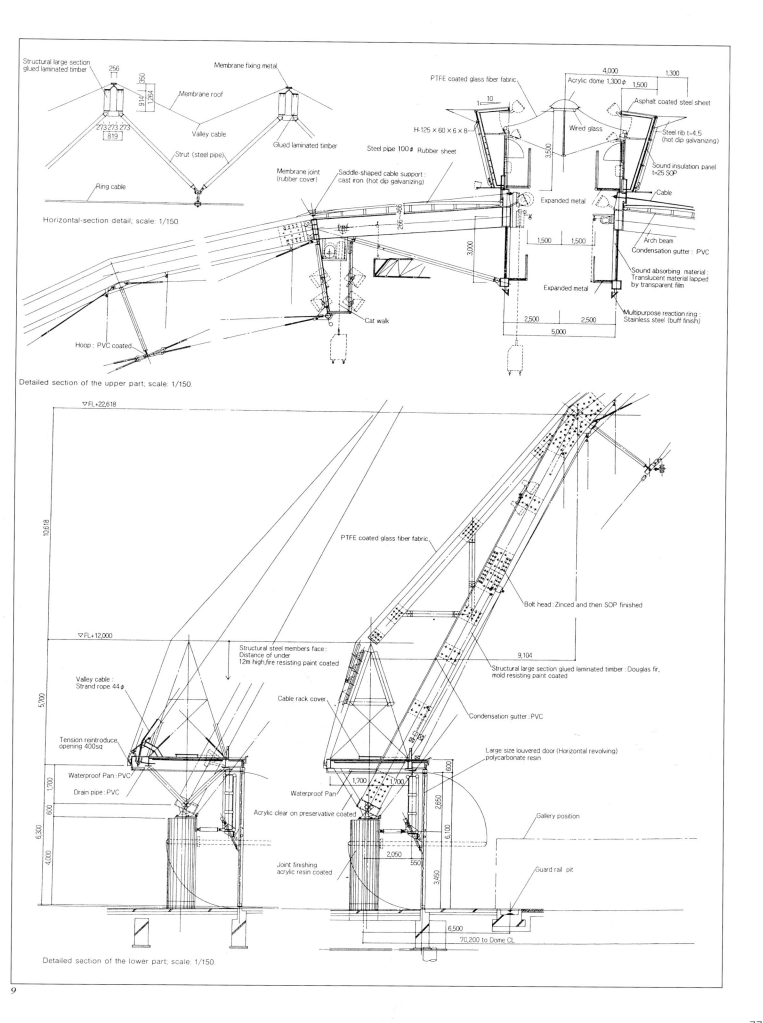

Structural large section glued laminated timber

Membrane fixing metal

Membrane roof

Valley cable

Strut (steel pipe)

Glued laminated timber

Ring cable

Horizontal-section detail; scale: 1/150.

PTFE coated glass fiber fabric

Acrylic dome 1,300 φ

Asphalt coated steel sheet

H-125 × 60 × 6 × 8

Wired glass

Steel rib t=4.5 (hot dip galvanizing)

Sound insulation panel t=25 SOP

Steel pipe 100 φ Rubber sheet

Membrane joint (rubber cover)

Saddle-shaped cable support : cast iron (hot dip galvanizing)

Expanded metal

Cable

Arch beam

Condensation gutter : PVC

Sound absorbing material : Translucent material lapped by transparent film

Expanded metal

Multipurpose reaction ring : Stainless steel (buff finish)

Cat walk

Hoop : PVC coated

Detailed section of the upper part; scale: 1/150.

▽FL+22,618

PTFE coated glass fiber fabric

Bolt head : Zinced and then SOP finished

▽FL+12,000

Structural steel members face : Distance of under 12m high, fire resisting paint coated

9,104

Structural large section glued laminated timber : Douglas fir, mold resisting paint coated

Valley cable : Strand rope 44 φ

Cable rack cover

Condensation gutter : PVC

Tension reintroduce opening 400sq

Large size louvered door (Horizontal revolving) polycarbonate resin

Waterproof Pan : PVC

Drain pipe : PVC

Waterproof Pan

Gallery position

Acrylic clear on preservative coated

Joint finishing acrylic resin coated

Guard rail pit

6,500

70,200 to Dome CL

Detailed section of the lower part; scale: 1/150.

9

ROOF

NAGANO OLYMPIC MEMORIAL ARENA, NAGANO, JAPAN
Kajima Design, Kume, Kajima, Okumura, Nissan, Iijima, Takagi Design Joint Venture

1

2

3

The greatest challenge of this project was to combine a wooden suspension roof and ceiling structure with an adjustable-space system – the first of its kind in the world.

The straight-line fixed stands will be used for large, post-Olympic events such as American football, while moveable, circular stands will function as walls and seating for smaller events such as concerts.

The remarkable Shinshu larch ceiling has imbued the interior with a soft fragrance and warmth that only wood can provide.

High U-value external wall and roof materials have reduced the heating load. A roof panelling system with a combination of glued-laminated timber and glass wool board has been included in the design to provide heating and noise insulation, sound absorption and fire prevention.

The suspended roof conserves energy by reducing the air volume of the space. A convex ceiling configuration makes it possible to achieve a clearer acoustic environment by diffusing the sound effectively through the whole arena.

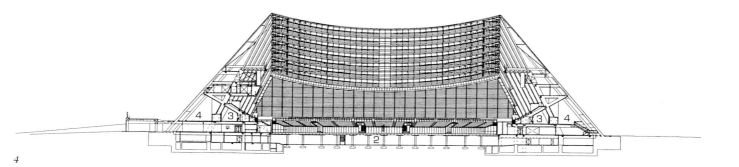

4

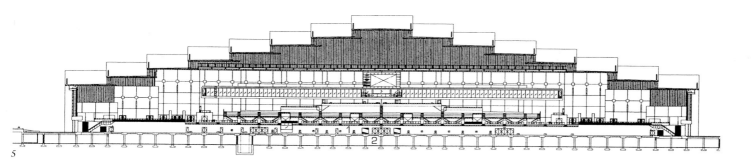

5

Evenly distributed ventilation openings and indirect roof lights (shading devices) installed between each roof layer, together with large glazed façades on both gable ends of the building, have provided a clean and comfortable indoor environment.

6

7

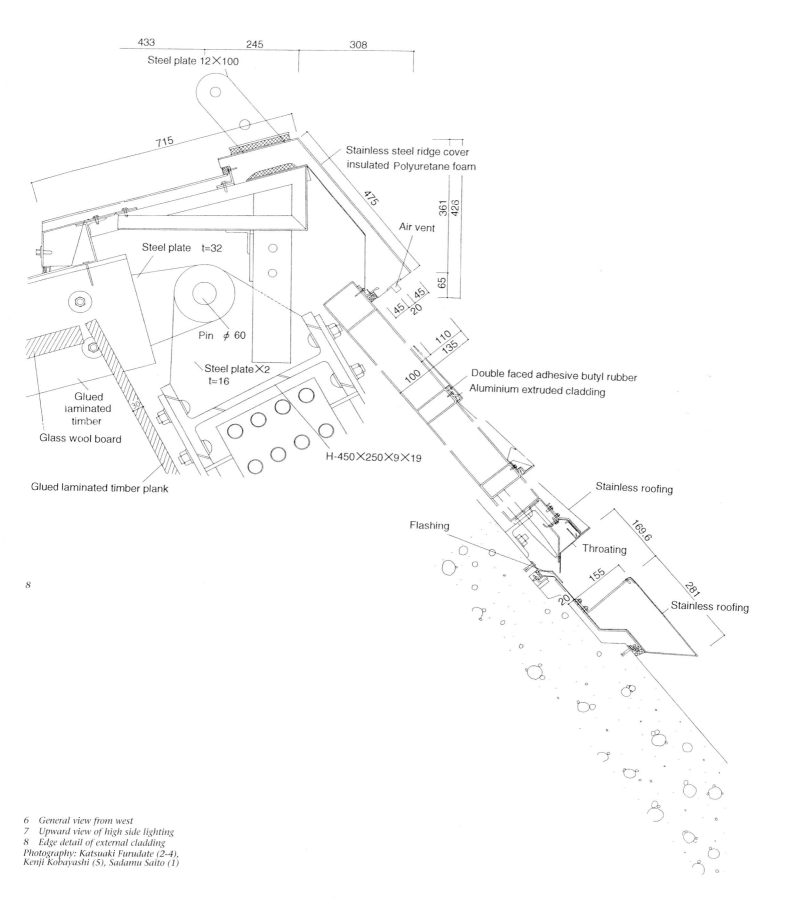

433   245   308

Steel plate 12×100

715

Stainless steel ridge cover
insulated Polyuretane foam

475

361
426

65

Air vent

Steel plate t=32

45 45
20

Pin φ 60

110
135

100

Steel plate×2
t=16

Double faced adhesive butyl rubber
Aluminium extruded cladding

Glued
laminated
timber

30

Glass wool board

H-450×250×9×19

Glued laminated timber plank

Stainless roofing

169.6

Flashing

Throating

155

281

20

Stainless roofing

8

6   General view from west
7   Upward view of high side lighting
8   Edge detail of external cladding
Photography: Katsuaki Furudate (2-4),
Kenji Kobayashi (5), Sadamu Saito (1)

SKYLIGHT, BRIDGE AND ACOUSTIC REFLECTION BOARD

SHINSHU OTANI-HA (HIGASHI HONGANJI) RECEPTION HALL, KYOTO, JAPAN

Kajima Design, Kansai   Design Supervisor: Shin Takamatsu

1

1   Night view of sun and moon-shaped
    skylight
2   Detailed section of skylight

The skylight of the vast Higashi Honganji underground temple of Kyoto was central to the design concept. It brings natural light and shadow into the space, consciously taking the scenery into the new frame of the building to develop new scenes. The addition to the temple was commissioned as part of the 500–year anniversary celebrations of Shen Buddhism revivalist Rennyo Shonin.

A large underground facility was designed with a skylight to be featured in the main existing site axis and to adopt a truncated cone form on the base. The skylight is the common feature of the three areas and creates a light garden open to the sky. The openings are meant to give visitors a sense of connection to the outside, leading them to recognise their own physical position and freedom from the closed place to support the idea of an open religious facility.

The walls of the exterior have been covered with acoustically designed inclining, folded, plate-wood board, creating a feeling of ascent and a feeling of relief, as if being held in Buddha's hand. The main exterior finish of the building is wood and reinforced concrete. By using natural materials, abstract and strong architectural form has been turned into a gentle image.

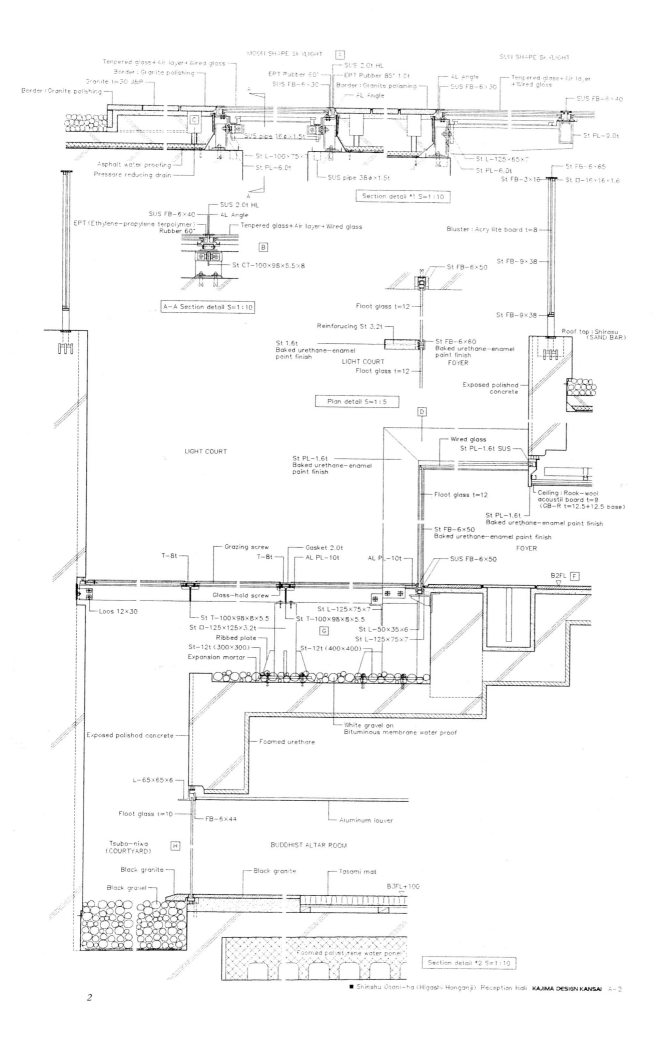

MOON SHAPE SKYLIGHT [A]

SUN SHAPE SKYLIGHT

Border : Granite polishing
Granite t=30 J&P
Border : Granite polishing
Tenpered glass+Air layer+Wired glass

SUS 2.0t HL
EPT Rubber 60°
EPT Rubber 85° 1.0t
SUS FB-6×30
Border : Granite polishing
AL Angle

AL Angle
SUS FB-6×30
Tenpered glass+Air layer+Wired glass
SUS FB-6×40

St PL-9.0t

Asphalt water proofing
Pressure reducing drain

SUS pipe 16∅×1.5t

St L-100×75×6
St PL-6.0t

SUS pipe 38∅×1.5t

St L-125×65×7
St PL-6.0t

St FB-6×65
St FB-3×16
St □-16×16×1.6

Section detail *1 S=1:10

SUS 2.0t HL
SUS FB-6×40
AL Angle
EPT (Ethylene-propylene terpolymer) Rubber 60°
Tenpered glass+Air layer+Wired glass

[B]

St CT-100×98×5.5×8

A-A Section detail S=1:10

Bluster : Acry lite board t=8

St FB-9×38

St FB-6×50

Floot glass t=12

Reinforucing St 3.2t
St 1.6t
Baked urethane-enamel paint finish

St FB-6×60
Baked urethane-enamel paint finish
FOYER

LIGHT COURT
Floot glass t=12

St FB-9×38

Roof top : Shirasu (SAND BAR)

Exposed polished concrete

Plan detail S=1:5

[D]

Wired glass
St PL-1.6t SUS

LIGHT COURT

St PL-1.6t
Baked urethane-enamel paint finish

Floot glass t=12

Ceiling : Rook-wool acoustil board t=9
(GB-R t=12.5+12.5 base)

St PL-1.6t
Baked urethane-enamel paint finish

St FB-6×50
Baked urethane-enamel paint finish

FOYER

Grazing screw
T-8t
Gasket 2.0t
T-8t
AL PL-10t
AL PL-10t
SUS FB-6×50

B2FL [F]

Glass-hold screw

Loos 12×30

St L-125×75×7

St T-100×98×8×5.5
St T-100×98×8×5.5
St □-125×125×3.2t
[G]
St L-50×35×6
St L-125×75×7
Ribbed plate
St-12t (300×300)
St-12t (400×400)
St L-125×75×7
Expansion mortar

White gravel on
Bituminous membrane water proof

Exposed polished concrete
Foamed urethane

L-65×65×6

Floot glass t=10
FB-6×44
Aluminum louver

Tsubo-niwa (COURTYARD) [H]
BUDDHIST ALTAR ROOM

Black granite
Black granite
Tatami mat

Black gravel
B3FL+100

B3FL+100

Foamed polystyrene water panel

Section detail *2 S=1:10

■ Shinshu Otani-ha (Higashi Honganji) Reception Hall **KAJIMA DESIGN KANSAI** A-2

2

3 *Upward view of moon-shaped skylight*
4 *Foyer*
5 *Acoustic reflection board on audiovisual hall wall*

3

4

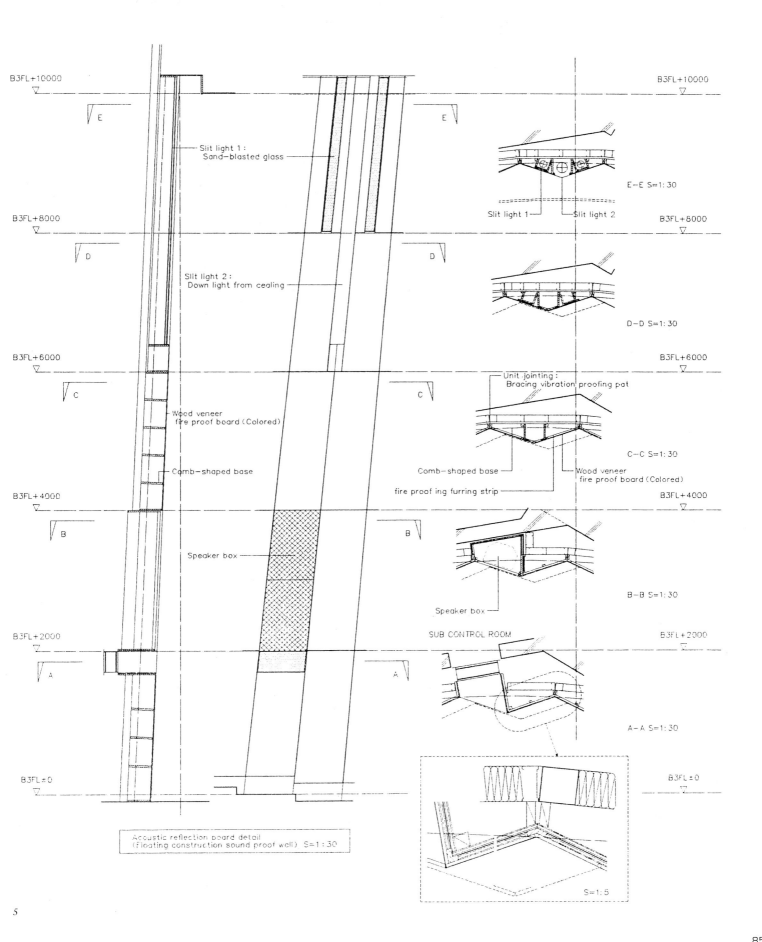

B3FL+10000

E

Slit light 1:
Sand-blasted glass

E-E S=1:30

Slit light 1 ——— Slit light 2

B3FL+8000

D

Slit light 2:
Down light from cealing

D-D S=1:30

B3FL+6000

C

Unit jointing:
Bracing vibration proofing pat

Wood veneer
fire proof board (Colored)

Comb-shaped base

C-C S=1:30

Comb-shaped base

Wood veneer
fire proof board (Colored)

fire proof ing furring strip

B3FL+4000

B

Speaker box

B-B S=1:30

Speaker box

B3FL+2000

SUB CONTROL ROOM

A

A-A S=1:30

B3FL±0

Acoustic reflection board detail
(Floating construction sound proof wall) S=1:30

S=1:5

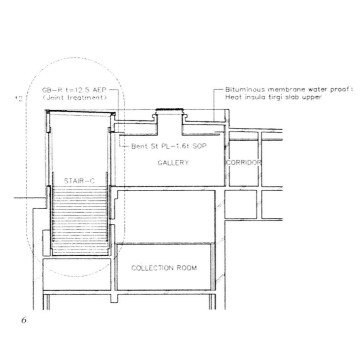

GB−R t=12.5 AEP (Joint treatment)

Bituminous membrane water proof: Heat insula tirgi slab upper

Bent St PL−1.6t SOP

GALLERY

CORRIDOR

STAIR−C

COLLECTION ROOM

6

7

I

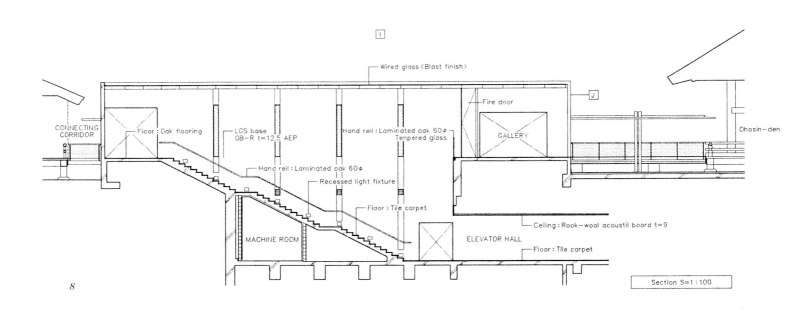

Wired glass (Blast finish)

J

CONNECTING CORRIDOR

Floor : Oak flooring

LGS base GB−R t=12.5 AEP

Hand reil : Laminated oak 60φ Tenpered glass

GALLERY

Ohosin−den

Hand reil : Laminated oak 60φ

Recessed light fixture

Fire door

Floor : Tile carpet

Ceiling : Rook−wool acoustil board t=9

MACHINE ROOM

ELEVATOR HALL

Floor : Tile carpet

Section S=1 : 100

8

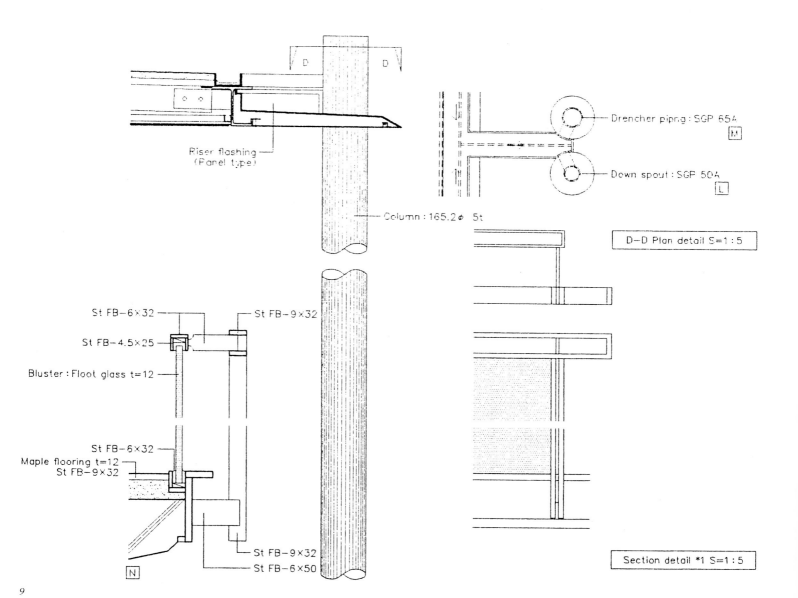

Riser flashing
(Panel type)

Drencher piping : SGP 65A [M]

Down spout : SGP 50A [L]

Column : 165.2 φ 5t

D-D Plan detail S=1:5

St FB-6×32

St FB-9×32

St FB-4.5×25

Bluster : Float glass t=12

St FB-6×32

Maple flooring t=12
St FB-9×32

St FB-9×32

St FB-6×50

[N]

Section detail *1 S=1:5

9

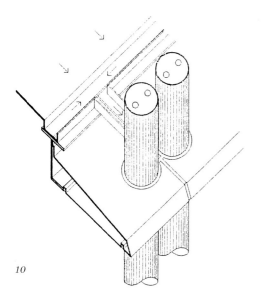

10

6 Plan showing stair
7 Night scene of staircase
8 Cross section showing staircase and handrail
9&10 Detail of bridge
Photography: Nacása & Partners inc.

PANEL WALL

NASU HISTORY MUSEUM, NASU, NASU-GUN, TOCHIGI PREFECTURE, JAPAN
Kengo Kuma & Associates

1

The Nasu History Museum is located in Ashino, Japan, an historic location along the main road during the Edo era. The museum was established to tell the rich history of the town of Nasu. The site contains a variety of historical elements, including a restored gate, old storehouse and a stone column from an elementary school. These items have been enclosed in a transparent glass building to keep them together.

Semi-transparent panels, made by attaching straw to aluminium mesh, are located behind the glass separating the building from the garden, thus enabling the exterior light to be controlled in a variety of ways.

Transparent partitions containing vines collected from nearby hills have been included at strategic locations to give the museum a unique ambience from the use of local materials.

The combination of transparent design with natural materials is called 'Sukiya'. The deployment of Sukiya in this design has created airiness and openness.

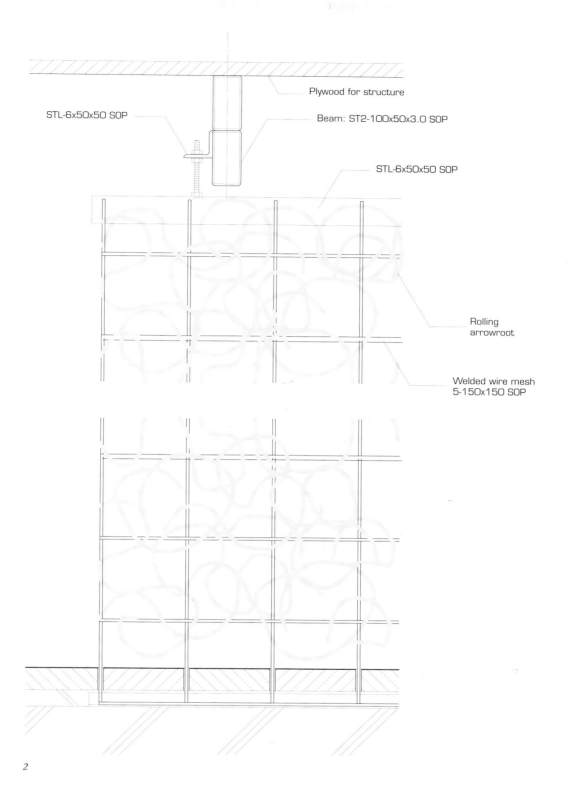

Plywood for structure

STL-6x50x50 SOP

Beam: ST2-100x50x3.0 SOP

STL-6x50x50 SOP

Rolling
arrowroot

Welded wire mesh
5-150x150 SOP

2

3

1 Entrance hall with rice paper wall and vine
   furniture
2 Elevation of panel wall
3 Moveable transparent panels with straw
   finish

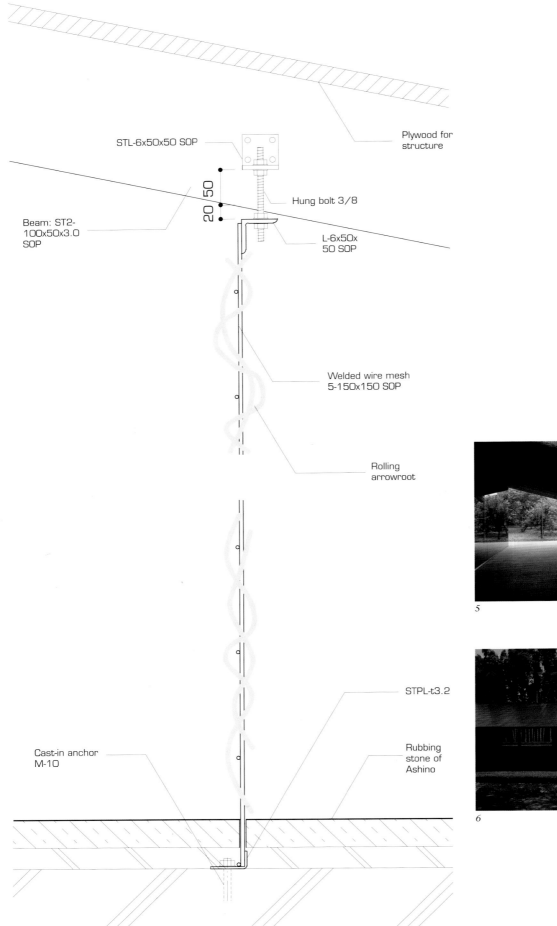

STL-6x50x50 SOP

Plywood for
structure

Hung bolt 3/8

Beam: ST2-
100x50x3.0
SOP

20 50

L-6x50x
50 SOP

Welded wire mesh
5-150x150 SOP

Rolling
arrowroot

STPL-t3.2

Cast-in anchor
M-10

Rubbing
stone of
Ashino

4

4   Side elevation of panel wall
5   Transparent exhibition room
6   Side view
7   Wara panel detail
8   Arrowroot panel detail
9   Garden view through glass
*Photography: courtesy Kengo Kuma &
Associates*

5

6

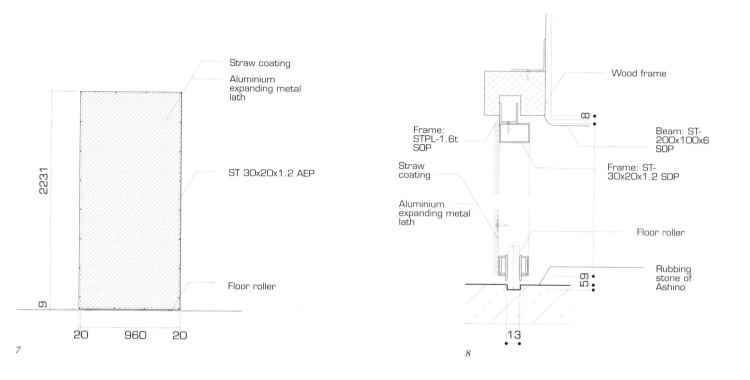

Straw coating

Aluminium
expanding metal
lath

ST 30x20x1.2 AEP

Floor roller

2231

9

20   960   20

7

Wood frame

Frame:
STPL-1.6t
SOP

Straw
coating

Aluminium
expanding metal
lath

8

Beam: ST-
200x100x6
SOP

Frame: ST-
30x20x1.2 SOP

Floor roller

Rubbing
stone of
Ashino

59

13

8

9

STONE WALL

NASU, NASU-GUN, TOCHIGI PREFECTURE, JAPAN
Kengo Kuma & Associates

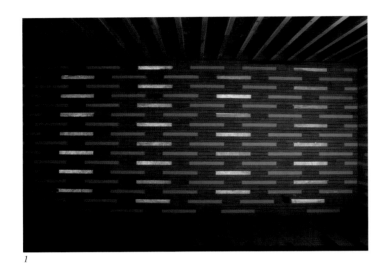

1

2

Beam:
St PL-19

Beam: St PL-12

Heat insulator waterproofing
Expanded polystyrene board
t=25 OSB t=25

Rafter
Bracket – vinyl
chloride holding
Cedar board

Marble

Local stone
(shirakawa stone)

Mortar

Surface of interior floor finish
Surface of exterior floor finish

Surface of water

4

3

The intention of the Stone Museum project was to recreate the three stone-based traditional Japanese storage buildings that were built long ago in the Ashino region of Nasu-city. The plan was to create a feeling of space with the introduction of passageways to create unification between the interior and its immediate environment.

The passageways have been built from two types of 'soft' walls. Stone is typically a heavy material that involves challenging processing methods. However, a sense of lightness, ambiguity and softness has been gained by de-solidifying the material with the inclusion of a series of slats or louvres.

Softness has also been achieved by punching numerous small openings in a stone-mounted wall. This has created an effect of ambiguity in the site boundary, and divided the light into infinite particles.

The contrast of softness experienced by the different treatments of stone and qualities of 'softness' can be remembered and re-experienced.

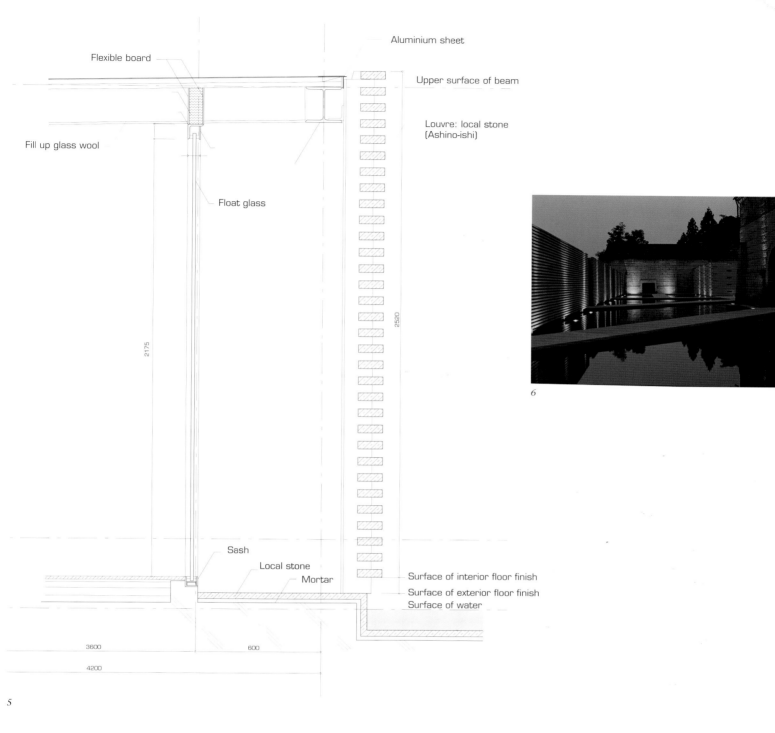

Aluminium sheet

Flexible board

Upper surface of beam

Louvre: local stone
(Ashino-ishi)

Fill up glass wool

Float glass

2175

2520

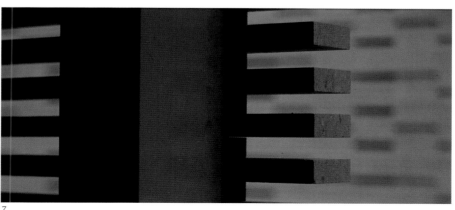
6

Sash

Local stone

Mortar

Surface of interior floor finish

Surface of exterior floor finish

Surface of water

3600   600

4200

5

1   Exhibition hall 1
2   Gallery 1
3   General eastern view
4   Sectional detail of wall
5   Sectional detail of louvres
6   Evening view
7   Detail of stone slats
*Photography: courtesy Kengo Kuma &
Associates*

7

CURTAINWALL

HOTEL KYOCERA, KAGOSHIMA PREFECTURE, JAPAN
Kisho Kurokawa Architect and Associates

1

The Hotel Kyocera was developed jointly by the towns of Kokubushi and Hayato. Located near the Kagoshima Airport, the hotel is an integrated element of the bustling Kagoshima *technopolis*; it accommodates the business traveller and the vacation traveller.

Simplicity is expressed in both the elliptical design and use of unpretentious precast concrete and glass. The central portion is a large atrium, spanning the full 60 metres of the building. Visually fusing with the exterior, the atrium space opens up dramatically as glass covers some 30 per cent of the roof and the entire southern exterior wall.

Circulation routes are separated into areas for guests and for those using the hotel's facilities, which include a banquet hall, sports complex and hot spring on the basement level; front lobby, restaurant and a tea lounge on the ground floor.

The guestrooms run along the building's exterior wall around the central void space. The corridor has been designed along the interior of the building. Through the skylight and glass section of the roof on the southern side natural light enters, brightening the dark and narrow corridors, creating a lighter, safer space.

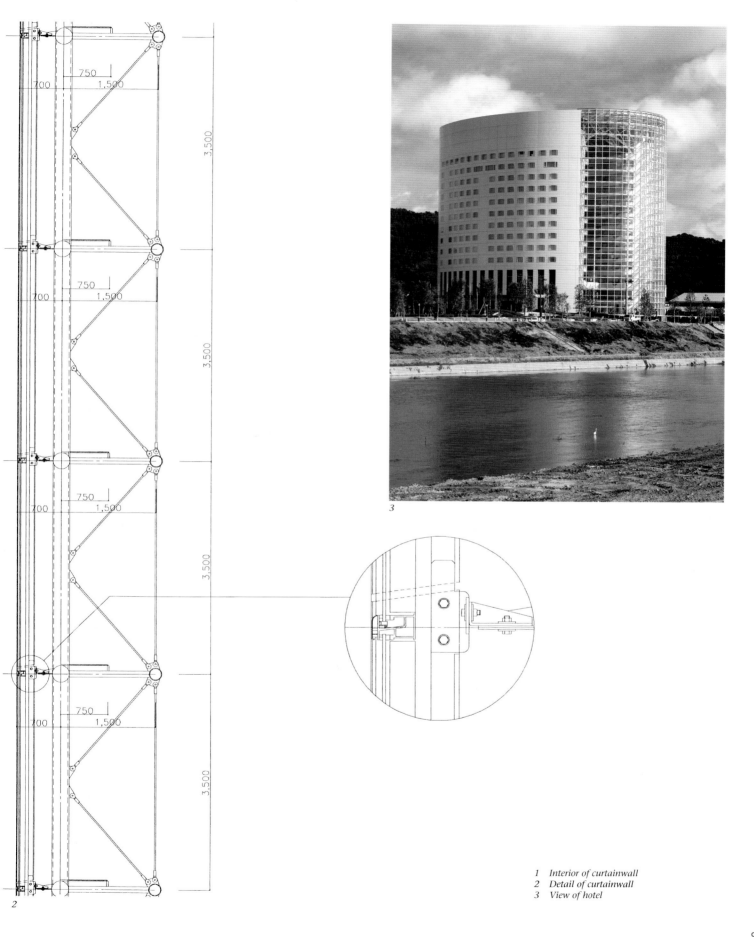

750
700
1,500

3,500

750
700
1,500

3,500

750
700
1,500

3,500

750
700
1,500

3,500

2

3

1 Interior of curtainwall
2 Detail of curtainwall
3 View of hotel

95

4

4&5   Interior view of curtainwall
  6   Section
  7   Site plan
Photography: Tomio Ohashi

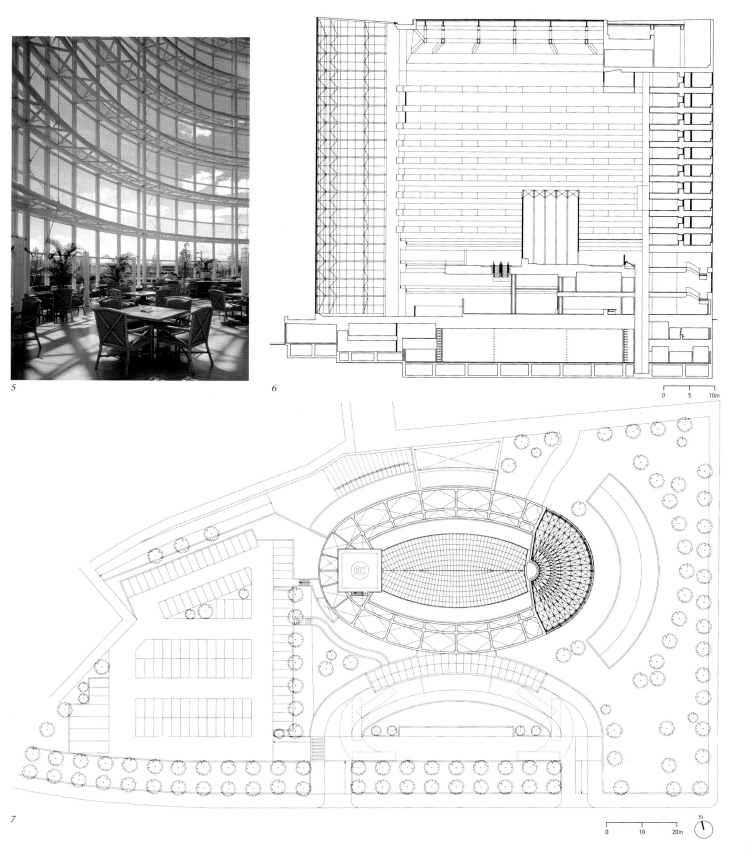

5

6

0   5   10m

7

0   10   20m

EAVES
WAKAYAMA PREFECTURAL MUSEUM AND THE MUSEUM OF MODERN ART, WAKAYAMA, JAPAN
Kisho Kurokawa Architect and Associates

1

2

The plan has been designed to correlate with the history of the site. The site was once the grounds of the ancient Wakayama Castle, but now houses the Wakayama Museum of Modern Art and the Wakayama Prefectural Museum.

The design features abstract versions of the traditional Japanese eave (Hisashi), paper-covered lamp stands (Andon), hanging lantern (Touro), folding screen (Byobu) and wall (Tsuijiber). Each has been manufactured with modern materials.

Four Andons have been placed at the corners of the recessed exterior wall. In addition, the inclusion in the design of single, double and triple eaves overlapping and appearing to float, create different expressions in each direction. Traditional appearance and modern materials have changed in symbiosis with the new generation.

3

1 Section
2 Eaves, lanterns, folding screens and walls
3 Eaves
4 Detail of eave

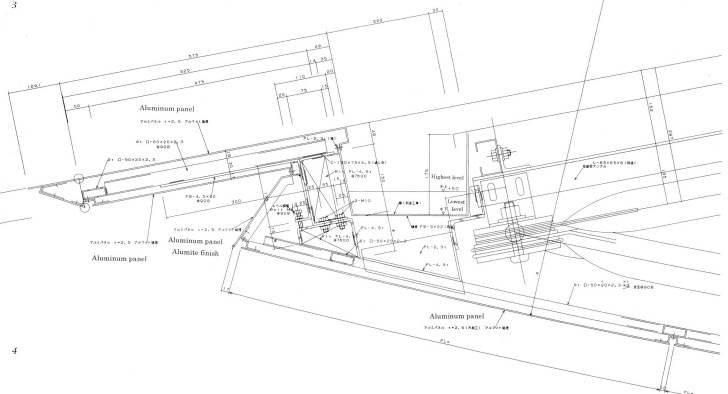

Aluminum panel

Aluminum panel

Aluminum panel
Alumite finish

Highest level

Lowest level

Aluminum panel

4

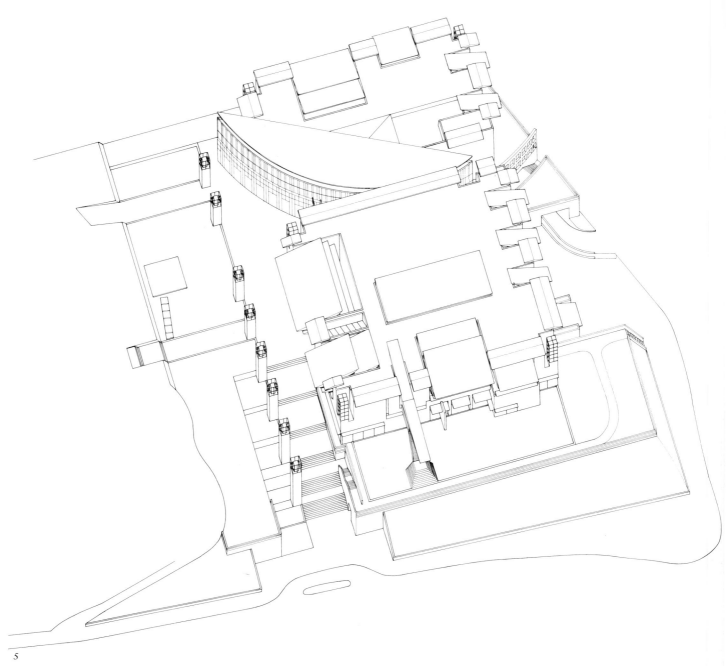

5

6

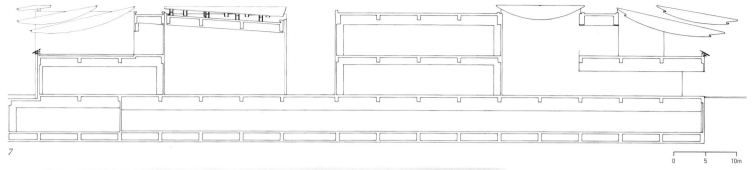

7

0 5 10m

5 Axonometric
6 Exterior view of Prefectural Museum
   at night
7 Section
8 Staircase
Photography: Tomio Ohashi

8

ATRIUM

CREW CENTRE EXTENSION, HELSINKI INTERNATIONAL AIRPORT, HELSINKI, FINLAND
KVA Architects LTD

1

1   *Illustration of atrium*
2   *Section*

The rectangular roof area on the third floor of the present six-storey steel-framed office building has been converted into an atrium. The atrium level will be a common meeting place during briefings, conferences and social functions. The atrium contains a 200-seat conference area with modern audiovisual equipment. The same area can also serve as a buffet if the furniture is changed. The surrounding office spaces of the old building and the extension join with two open stairs and galleries.

The inclined shape of the skylight follows the level of the eaves, or the present three-storey-high blue external glass wall and the new five-storey-high extension wall where blind areas are covered with acoustic sheeting. The primary load-bearing steel beams have been situated 7.2 metres apart with the secondary beams 1.8 metres apart. The size of the entire complex will be about 37,400 square metres and total volume around 156,000 cubic metres.

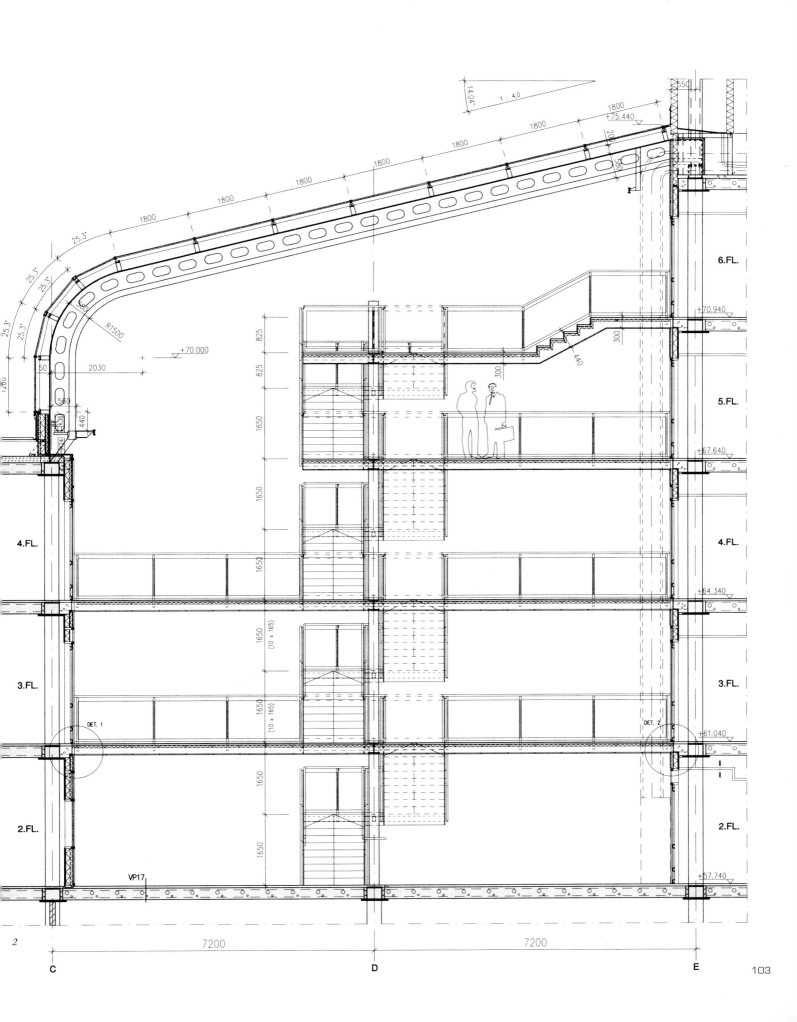

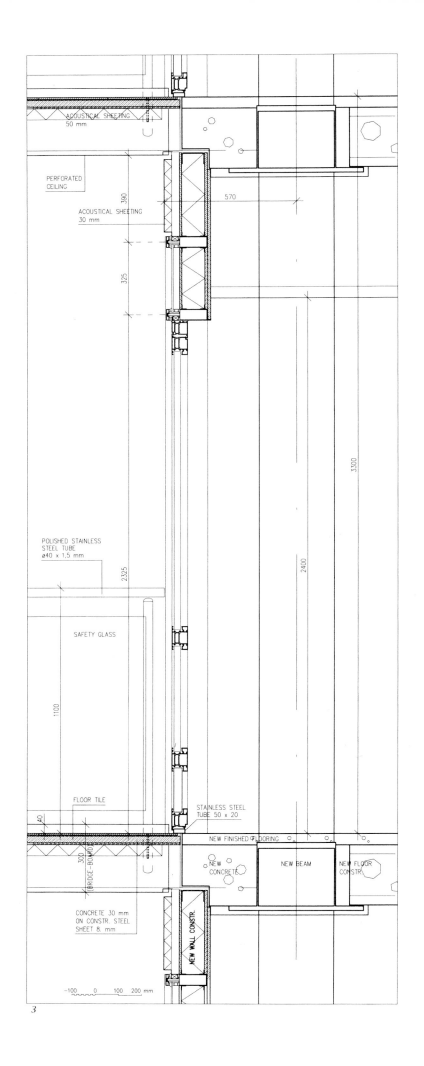

ACOUSTICAL SHEETING
50 mm

PERFORATED
CEILING

ACOUSTICAL SHEETING
30 mm

390

570

325

3300

POLISHED STAINLESS
STEEL TUBE
ø40 x 1,5 mm

2325

2400

SAFETY GLASS

1100

FLOOR TILE

40

STAINLESS STEEL
TUBE 50 x 20

NEW FINISHED FLOORING

300

(BRIDGE-BOARD)

NEW
CONCRETE

NEW BEAM

NEW FLOOR
CONSTR.

CONCRETE 30 mm
ON CONSTR. STEEL
SHEET 8. mm

NEW WALL CONSTR.

-100   0   100   200 mm

3

104

3   *Vertical details of gallery*
4   *Illustration from atrium level*
Photography: courtesy KVA Architects Ltd

4

CURTAINWALL

MULTILEVEL CAR PARK, P5, HELSINKI INTERNATIONAL AIRPORT, HELSINKI, FINLAND
KVA Architects LTD

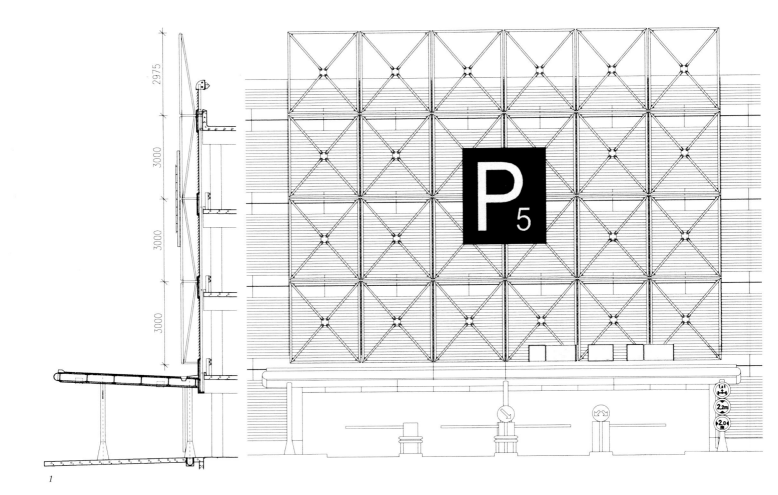

1

1 *Vertical section and façade of curtainwall*
2 *Façade structure of entrance area*
3 *Car park entrance*
4 *Section of the curtainwall*
5 *Entrance façade*
Photography: Jussi Tiainen

The car park with an area of 53,150 square metres and a volume of 143,265 cubic metres rests on a cast-in-situ cross-stiffened slab, with concrete columns placed about 15.8 metres, and beams 5 metres apart. The frame is divided into four sections, with expansion joints and a spiral ramp in the centre.

The slabs were poststressed within two days from casting. There are approximately 1,950 parking places in this seven-storey building which is connected by a tunnel with the neighbouring staff facility, the Crew Centre.

The three lower parking levels for the airport passengers, situated underground, are equipped with mechanical ventilation and an automatic fire extinguisher. The four upper levels have natural ventilation through the external curtainwall and the open ramp area.

The curtainwall consists of curved horizontal louvres designed for this building. The extruded, powder-coated, silver-grey aluminium louvres, placed 100 millimetres apart, are supported by aluminium assembly units screwed on the vertical profiles. The cars parked inside the building are

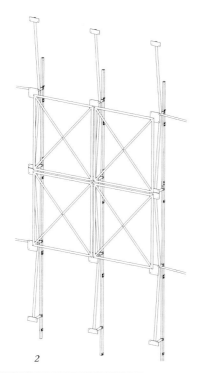

2

3

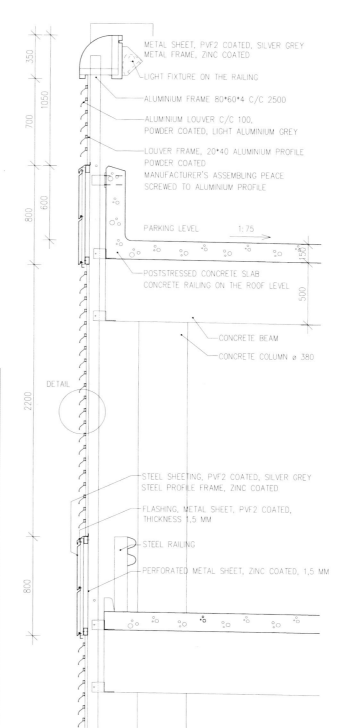

METAL SHEET, PVF2 COATED, SILVER GREY
METAL FRAME, ZINC COATED

LIGHT FIXTURE ON THE RAILING

ALUMINIUM FRAME 80*60*4 C/C 2500

ALUMINIUM LOUVER C/C 100,
POWDER COATED, LIGHT ALUMINIUM GREY

LOUVER FRAME, 20*40 ALUMINIUM PROFILE
POWDER COATED
MANUFACTURER'S ASSEMBLING PEACE
SCREWED TO ALUMINIUM PROFILE

PARKING LEVEL   1:75

POSTSTRESSED CONCRETE SLAB
CONCRETE RAILING ON THE ROOF LEVEL

CONCRETE BEAM

CONCRETE COLUMN ø 380

DETAIL

STEEL SHEETING, PVF2 COATED, SILVER GREY
STEEL PROFILE FRAME, ZINC COATED

FLASHING, METAL SHEET, PVF2 COATED,
THICKNESS 1,5 MM

STEEL RAILING

PERFORATED METAL SHEET, ZINC COATED, 1,5 MM

4

effectively hidden behind the blind linear areas covered with PVF2-coated steel-sheeting. The external wall has a light aluminium frame.

The entrance area for the passenger driveway has been emphasised by a four-storey-high steel structure, with a façade frame constructed of welded brush-polished stainless steel tubes. The entrance canopy shelters the ticket vending units and barriers, and stainless steel is the basic material used in all canopy-style structures of this building.

5

WALL AND HANDRAIL

THE WHANKI MUSEUM, SEOUL, KOREA

Kyu Sung Woo Architect, Inc

1

2

This private foundation is dedicated to the memory and spirit of the contemporary Korean painter, Kim Whanki. The program reflects his spirit as a cultural centre and gathering place for artists. Galleries for paintings and temporary exhibitions have been combined with a small cafe, director's office and a main hall to form the museum's social structure. Each of these programmatic elements is contained in a separate building volume.

The forms have been organised along an east–west line to reflect the direction of the dominant mountain valley in which the museum is located.

The volumes are linked by interior and exterior circulation paths and terraces that traverse the settlement of the steep hillside.

To house the extensive program and maintain a balance between open space, new building and the surrounding neighbourhood, many program spaces are located underground. The interior space of the museum has been formed around an eight-metre cube, located below an exterior courtyard. This space accommodates exhibitions and assembly functions as well as other activities. It is the museum's centre of circulation and orientation.

1   Central hall from second floor
2   Vitrail from second floor
3&4 Main stair handrail detail
5   Section through Central Hall wall
Photography: Timothy Hursley

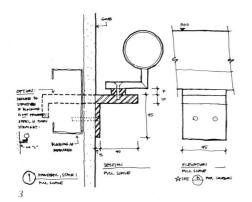

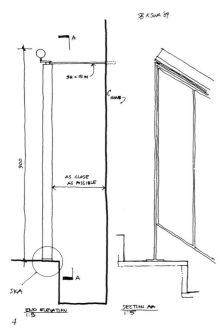

Each exhibition space is connected by staircases that surround this plaza. The exterior walls of these staircases are washed by daylight to relieve the confined feeling of being underground. At the centre of the complex and at the beginning of the staircases to the east lies a deep, dark pond of water that enhances a primal image of light, water and containment underground.

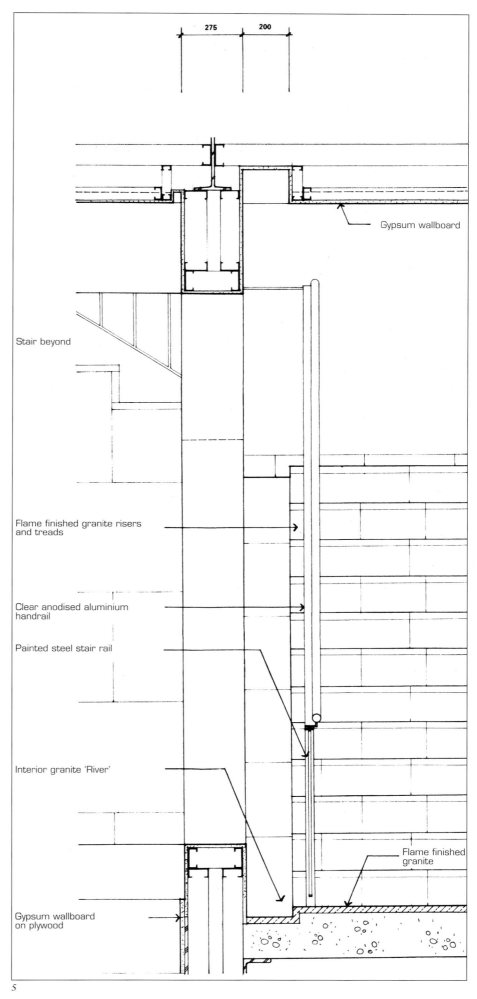

Gypsum wallboard

Stair beyond

Flame finished granite risers and treads

Clear anodised aluminium handrail

Painted steel stair rail

Interior granite 'River'

Flame finished granite

Gypsum wallboard on plywood

5

PODIUM, GLAZED ROOF AND MOTOR-CONTROLLED FABRIC SUNSHADE

KADOORIE BIOLOGICAL SCIENCES BUILDING, THE UNIVERSITY OF HONG KONG, HONG KONG SAR, PRC
Leigh and Orange Ltd

1

2

1 *Inverted pyramid support structure*
2 *Glazed entrance lobby*
3 *Plan of glazed entrance canopy*
4 *Section*

The design for the building has met the combined demands of a highly constrained site while still providing functionality, flexibility, safety, energy efficiency, environmental friendliness, lifetime economy, sustainability, buildability and ease of maintenance.

It contains eight storeys of laboratories comprising two identically sized laboratory suites per floor, planned either side of a central circulation core housing toilet, lifts and main staircase. Teaching laboratories are located in the two lower floors and the upper six floors are for research laboratory functions. The remaining top floors have been taken up with ancillary facilities of greenhouses

and aquaria, plantrooms and space for building services.

The covered podium level acts as a dedicated pedestrian circulation concourse linking the building to the overall campus circulation pattern and providing a main entrance level from that pedestrian access can be gained to the building.

The classical symmetry responds to the orthogonal planning discipline of the campus in which it sits and echoes, in modern idiom, the neoclassical main building, which was designed by the same firm in 1912.

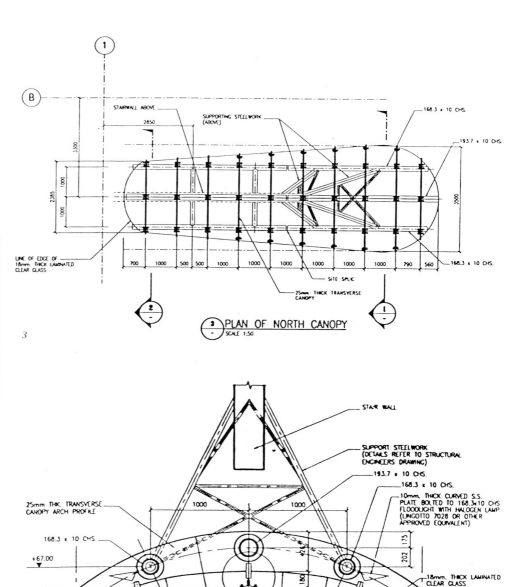

SUPPORTING STEELWORK
(ABOVE)

STAIRWALL ABOVE

2850

168.3 x 10 CHS.

193.7 x 10 CHS.

LINE OF EDGE OF
18mm THICK LAMINATED
CLEAR GLASS

700 | 1000 | 500 | 500 | 1000 | 1000 | 1000 | 1000 | 1000 | 1000 | 790 | 560

168.3 x 10 CHS.

SITE SPLICE

25mm THICK TRANSVERSE
CANOPY

3 PLAN OF NORTH CANOPY
SCALE 1:50

3

STAIR WALL

SUPPORT STEELWORK
(DETAILS REFER TO STRUCTURAL
ENGINEERS DRAWING)

193.7 x 10 CHS.

168.3 x 10 CHS.

10mm THICK CURVED S.S.
PLATE BOLTED TO 168.3x10 CHS
FLOODLIGHT WITH HALOGEN LAMP
(UNGOTTO 7028 OR OTHER
APPROVED EQUIVALENT)

25mm THK. TRANSVERSE
CANOPY ARCH PROFILE

168.3 x 10 CHS.

+67.00

1000 | 1000

18mm. THICK LAMINATED
CLEAR GLASS

450 MAX

VARIES

1075

1075

VARIES

R=2000

R=2750

R=5399

R=2000

3500 MAX

3595

1 SECTION
SCALE 1:20

4

The elegant simplicity of the architectural solution belies its intellectual depth. The adoption of a space-efficient, deep-plan, shell and core planning approach, utilising demountable partitioning, grided overhead services, modular laboratory furniture, and a state-of-the-art fume cupboard design has allowed the creation of a remarkably flexible building. Furthermore, easily accessed, externally located building services prevent the contamination of sensitive spaces by maintenance personnel and offers safe, easy maintenance at all times.

The application of recirculatory type fume cupboards, double skin arrangement for solar control, and locations equipment with heat emission in the external services zone, it is estimated to achieve energy saving of 44.1 million Kilowatt-hours, and to reduce the emission of carbon dioxide by 26.9 million tonnes over the assumed 50-year lifetime of the building.

111

5

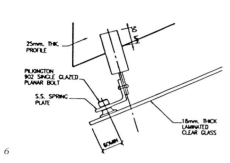

25mm. THK.
PROFILE

PILKINGTON
902 SINGLE GLAZED
PLANAR BOLT

S.S. SPRING
PLATE

18mm. THICK
LAMINATED
CLEAR GLASS

6

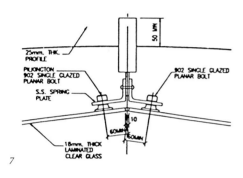

25mm. THK.
PROFILE

PILKINGTON
902 SINGLE GLAZED
PLANAR BOLT

902 SINGLE GLAZED
PLANAR BOLT

S.S. SPRING
PLATE

18mm. THICK
LAMINATED
CLEAR GLASS

7

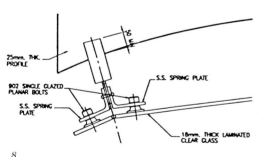

25mm. THK.
PROFILE

902 SINGLE GLAZED
PLANAR BOLTS

S.S. SPRING PLATE

S.S. SPRING
PLATE

18mm. THICK LAMINATED
CLEAR GLASS

8

5   Glazed entrance lobby
6,7&8   Fixing detail of glazed entrance lobby
9   South façade
10   Podium concourse
11   Diagrammatic cross section

9

10

11

113

12

13

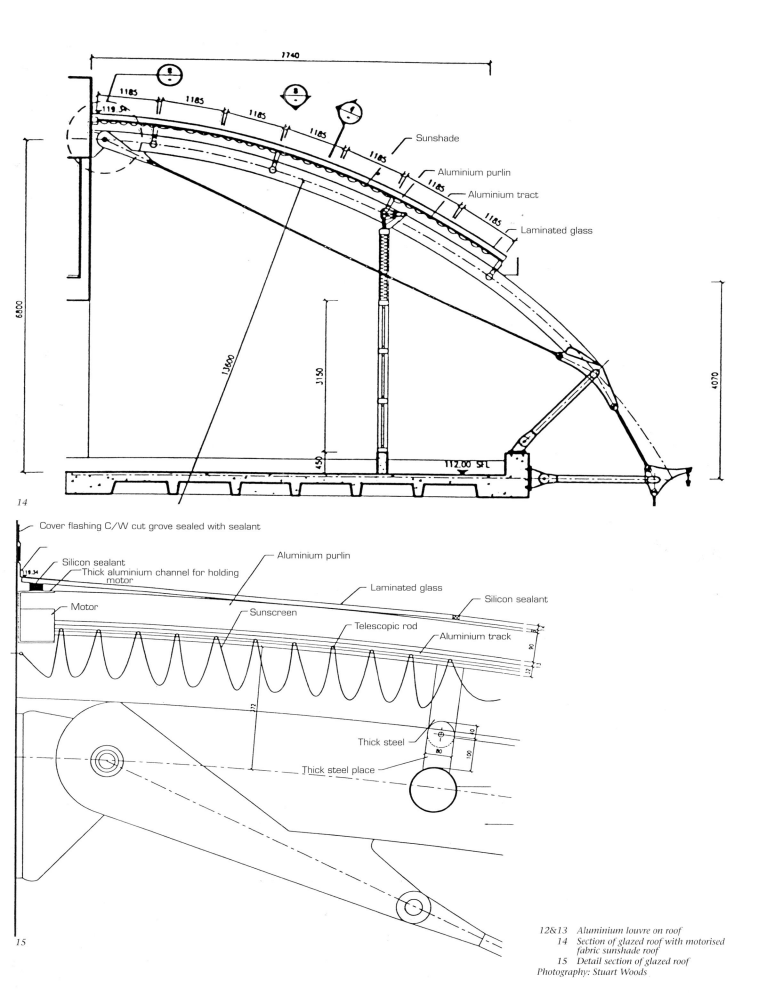

1740

1185
1185
1185
1185
1185
1185

119.5

Sunshade

Aluminium purlin

Aluminium tract

Laminated glass

6800

13800

3150

450

112.00 SFL

4070

14

Cover flashing C/W cut grove sealed with sealant

Silicon sealant
Thick aluminium channel for holding motor

119.34

Aluminium purlin

Laminated glass

Silicon sealant

Motor

Sunscreen

Telescopic rod

Aluminium track

90

272

Thick steel

10

80

100

Thick steel place

15

12&13   Aluminium louvre on roof
14   Section of glazed roof with motorised
        fabric sunshade roof
15   Detail section of glazed roof
Photography: Stuart Woods

GLASS PANEL SCREEN
MARTIN SHOCKET RESIDENCE, CHEVY CHASE, MARYLAND, USA
McInturff Architects

1

2

1&2   Panel frames
  3   Detail of panel frame
Photography: Julia Heine

When our clients bought their 1920s foursquare catalogue house in an older suburb of Washington DC, they discovered a one-storey building of equal footprint in the backyard. Built as a photographer's studio, but never used after the neighbours complained, it was marginally connected to the house by a hyphen that resolved a half-level change. The job of the architect was to integrate this room into the life of the house and the family.

The room was opened to the garden through a new wall of steel-framed windows and doors leading to a new porch. A new structural system creates both the openings and a cantilevered

canopy shading the porch. Pairs of steel columns, one within the wall and the other slightly inside it, support the canopy and are joined by panels of sandblasted glass to reflect oblique light into the space. The inner columns are softened to the touch and the eye by cherrywood cladding.

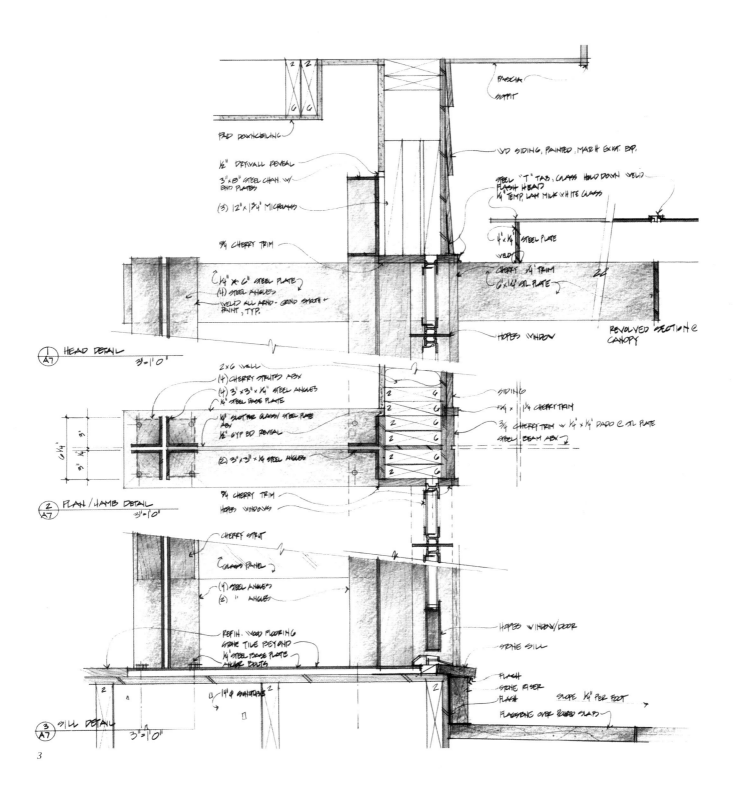

HEAD DETAIL ①/A7 3"=1'0"

PLAN/JAMB DETAIL ②/A7 3"=1'0"

SILL DETAIL ③/A7 3"=1'0"

FRD DOWNCEILING

½" DRYWALL REVEAL
3"×8" STEEL CHAN. W/ END PLATES
(3) 12"×1¾" MICROLAMS

¾ CHERRY TRIM

(¼" × 6" STEEL PLATE
(4) STEEL ANGLES
WELD ALL ARND - GRIND SMOOTH + PAINT, TYP.

FASCIA
SOFFIT

WD SIDING, PAINTED, MATCH EXIST. BP.
STEEL "T" TAB, GLASS HOLD DOWN WELD FLASH HEAD
¼" TEMP LAM MILK WHITE GLASS
¼" × ¼" STEEL PLATE
WELD
CHERRY ¼" TRIM
6"×1¼" STL. PLATE

HOPES WINDOW

REVOLVED SECTION CANOPY

2×6 WALL
(4) CHERRY STRUTS ABV
(4) 3"×3"×¼" STEEL ANGLES
¼" STEEL BASE PLATE
¼" SLOTTED GLASS/STEEL PLATE ABV
½" GYP ED REVEAL

(2) 3"×3"×¼ STEEL ANGLES

¾ CHERRY TRIM
HOPES WINDOWS

SIDING
¾ × 1¼ CHERRY TRIM
¾ CHERRY TRIM W ¼" × ¼" DADO @ STL PLATE
STEEL BEAM ABV

CHERRY STRUT
GLASS PANEL
(4) STEEL ANGLES
(2) " ANGLES

REFIN. WOOD FLOORING
STONE TILE BEYOND
¼" STEEL BASE PLATE
ANCHOR BOLTS

1¼" Ø ANCHORS

HOPES WINDOW/DOOR
STONE SILL
FLASH
STONE RISER
FLASH
SLOPE ¼" PER FOOT
FLAGSTONE OVER POURED SLAB

3

STAIR
HUTNER STAIR, CHEVY CHASE, MARYLAND, USA
McInturff Architects

1

1 Family room
2 Detail of landing and stringer connections
3 Stair plan and elevation

As part of a project that involved transforming a small house from one storey into two, an obvious requirement was the making of a stair. The introduction of a new significant element into the plan seemed to be an opportunity to focus on the stair as a unique event, so it was designed as a removable bridge between a stone landing at the bottom and a wooden platform at the top. In a sense, it is a 'gangplank' of the sort used to span between a dock and the deck of an ocean liner, and can be installed or removed as a self-sufficient structure.

The stair is laid into steel shoes at the top and bottom, but is otherwise attached to adjacent surfaces only by the handrail. Structurally, the stringer is made from a series of spaced maple planks, bolted together, through which various steel elements pass, including the handrail and tread supports and king post truss elements. Maple is used for parts that are either touched – treads and handrails – or in compression, such as stringers.

Steel is used for connections, rail structural elements and the elements in tension, such as the truss post-tensioning rod.

Should the clients ever move to another house, it is suspected that they will take the stair with them.

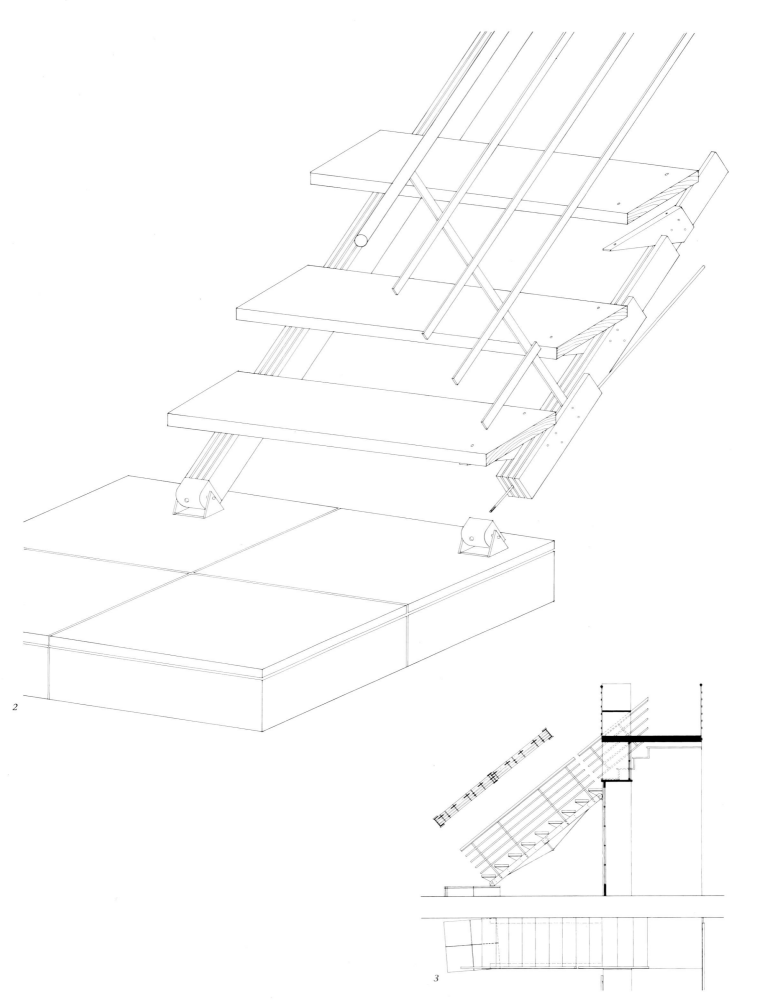

2

3

119

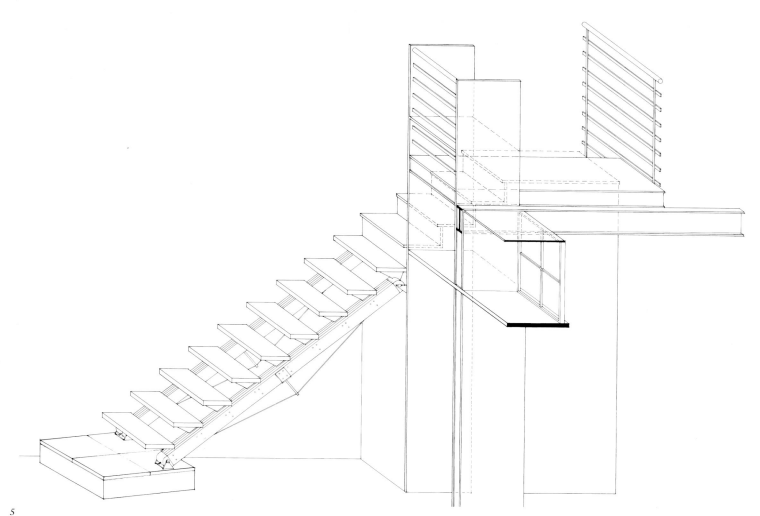

5

6

Opposite:
  Detail
5 *Axonometric of stair and second floor*
   landing
6 *Stair to new second floor*
Photography: Julia Heine

STAIRS

KING STAIRS, CHEVY CHASE, MARYLAND, USA
McInturff Architects

1

2

1   *View from second floor landing*
2   *Detail*
3   *Detail of connections*
4   *View from third floor landing*
Photography: Julia Heine

As part of a larger renovation and addition to an existing 1920s house, a new stair was required to access a new third floor. The stair was taken both literally and figuratively to be the centre of the project, and the new piece reflects the transition from the traditional language of the original space to the more modern aesthetic of the addition. Starting opposite the front door in this centre hall house, only the railing design hints at what follows.

At the second floor landing, the solidity of the lower run gives way to an open stair, detailed with a minimalist profile and open risers to allow light from above to penetrate the stair, and light the entry below. Wooden plank treads join with steel rods, channels and cables to create a visual and tactile contrast.

At the top landing, these planks continue as a cantilevered gallery to provide access to new third floor rooms.

Gaps between the boards, between landing and wall, and between stair treads allow light to filter below and help articulate the pieces of this kit-of-parts approach.

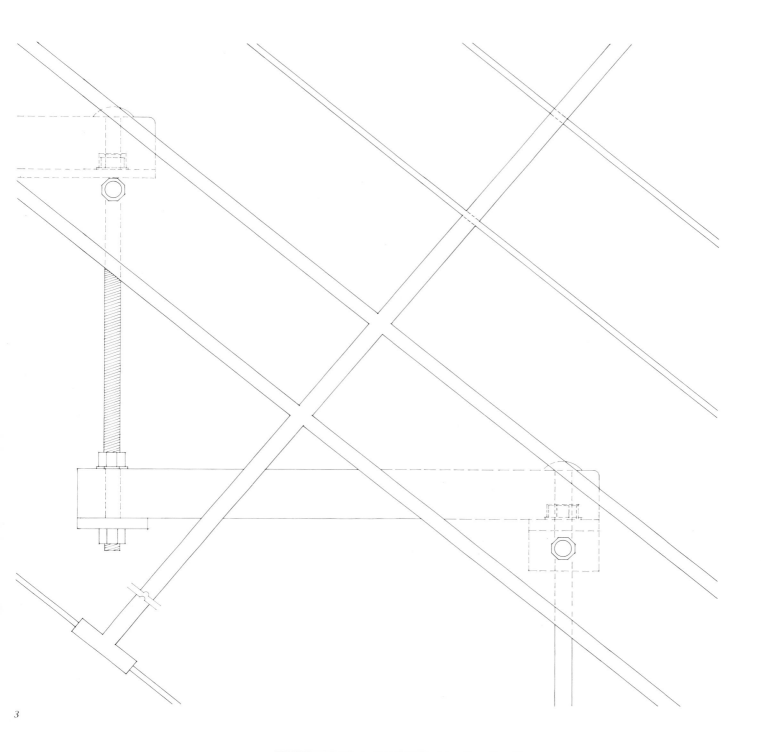

3

4

123

CONSERVATORY
BLAKES RESTAURANT, SOUTHGATE, MELBOURNE, AUSTRALIA
Maddison Architects

1

Blakes Restaurant was created when Melbourne's Southgate complex was opened. It was extensively renovated and extended in 1999. The recently added dining room or 'conservatory' on the western side, is supported by five 'coat hanger' steel rectangular hollow sections. As a result of the stringent access requirements imposed by service authorities to underground infrastructure, this new addition needed to be completely demountable. These conditions are reflected in the detailing and construction.

The idea of the roof floating above a mullion-free window system was pursued to capture the view. The overall 'conservatory' structure is a kit of parts

that can be sequentially demounted. It consists of steel-roof support arms, lightweight roofing steel, window system and precast base dwarf wall.

All elements of the structure can be easily undone and hoisted from the site by a single crane. The externally expressed steel support arms are connected to the main façade and base dwarf wall by removable pin joint connections

Overall, the new addition has met the expanded needs of the client whilst satisfying the difficult access requirements of service authorities. The result is a dynamic structure that creates a dramatic sense of arrival at the restaurant.

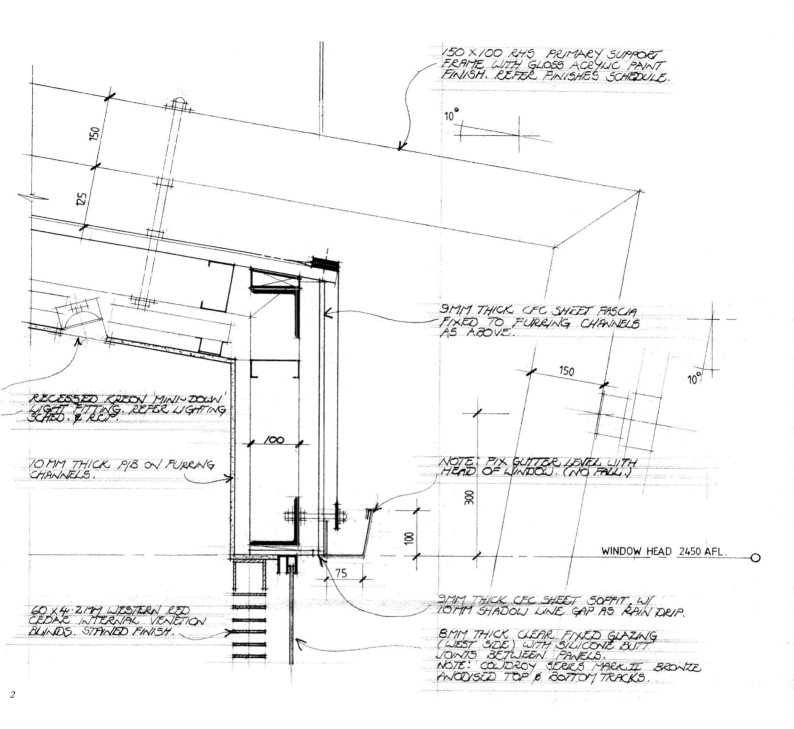

150 × 100 RHS PRIMARY SUPPORT
FRAME WITH GLOSS ACRYLIC PAINT
FINISH. REFER FINISHES SCHEDULE.

10°

150

125

9MM THICK CFC SHEET FASCIA
FIXED TO FURRING CHANNELS
AS ABOVE.

150

10°

RECESSED KREON 'MINI-DOWN'
LIGHT FITTING. REFER LIGHTING
SCHED. & RCP.

100

NOTE: FIX GUTTER LEVEL WITH
HEAD OF WINDOW. (NO FALL.)

300

10MM THICK P/B ON FURRING
CHANNELS.

100

WINDOW HEAD 2450 AFL.

75

9MM THICK CFC SHEET SOFFIT W/
10MM SHADOW LINE GAP AS RAIN DRIP.

60 × 4·2MM WESTERN RED
CEDAR INTERNAL VENETIAN
BLINDS. STAINED FINISH.

8MM THICK CLEAR FIXED GLAZING
(WEST SIDE) WITH SILICONE BUTT
JOINTS BETWEEN PANELS.
NOTE: COWDROY SERIES MARK II BRONZE
ANODISED TOP & BOTTOM TRACKS.

2

1 Melbourne skyline and Blakes Restaurant
2 Section through wall/ceiling junction
3 Open kitchen and bar

3

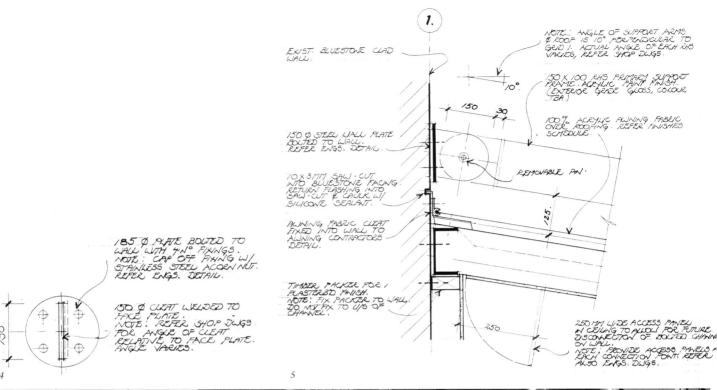

1.

EXIST. BLUESTONE CLAD WALL.

NOTE: ANGLE OF SUPPORT ARMS & ROOF IS 10° PERPENDICULAR TO GRID 1. ACTUAL ANGLE OF EACH RHS VARIES, REFER SHOP DWGS.

10°

150 X 100 RHS PRIMARY SUPPORT FRAME. ACRYLIC PAINT FINISH. (EXTERIOR GRADE GLOSS, COLOUR TBA).

150   30

150 Ø STEEL WALL PLATE BOLTED TO WALL. REFER ENGS. DETAIL.

100% ACRYLIC AWNING FABRIC OVER ROOFING. REFER FINISHES SCHEDULE.

10 X 3MM SAW-CUT INTO BLUESTONE FACING. RETURN FLASHING INTO SAW-CUT & CAULK W/ SILICONE SEALANT.

REMOVABLE PIN.

125.

AWNING FABRIC CLEAT FIXED INTO WALL TO AWNING CONTRACTORS DETAIL.

185 Ø PLATE BOLTED TO WALL WITH 4 N° FIXINGS. NOTE: CAP OFF FIXING W/ STAINLESS STEEL ACORN NUT. REFER ENGS. DETAIL.

TIMBER PACKER FOR PLASTERB'D FINISH. NOTE: FIX PACKER TO WALL, DO NOT FIX TO U/S OF CHANNEL.

150 Ø CLEAT WELDED TO FACE PLATE. NOTE: REFER SHOP DWGS FOR ANGLE OF CLEAT RELATIVE TO FACE PLATE. ANGLE VARIES.

250

150

250 MM WIDE ACCESS PANEL IN CEILING TO ALLOW FOR FUTURE DISCONNECTION OF BOLTED CHANNEL ON WALL. NOTE: PROVIDE ACCESS PANELS AT EACH CONNECTION POINT, REFER ALSO ENGS. DWGS.

4   5

6

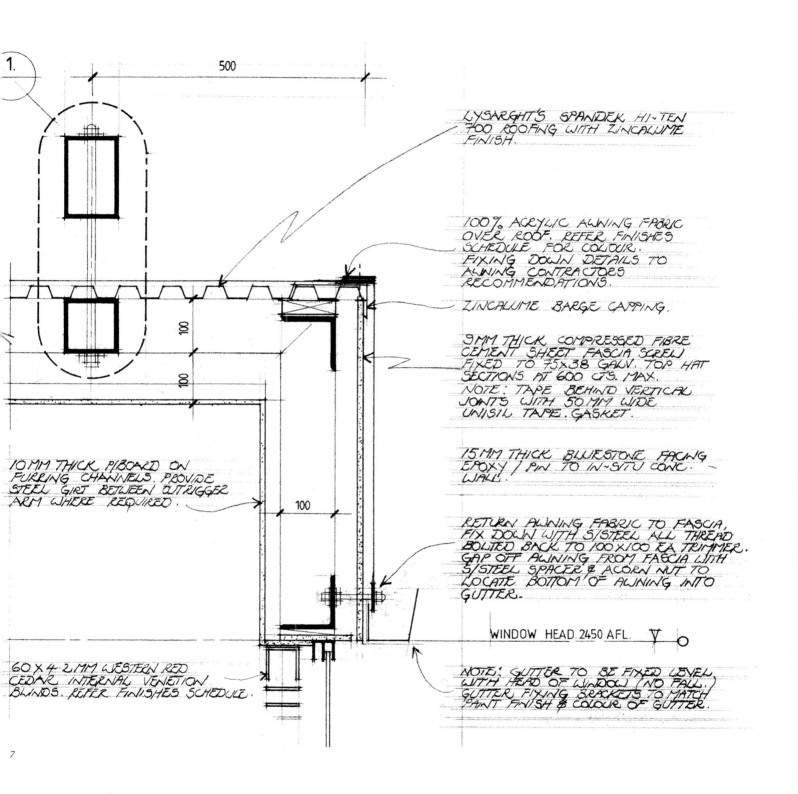

1.

500

100

100

100

LYSAGHT'S SPANDEK HI-TEN 700 ROOFING WITH ZINCALUME FINISH.

100% ACRYLIC AWNING FABRIC OVER ROOF. REFER FINISHES SCHEDULE FOR COLOUR. FIXING DOWN DETAILS TO AWNING CONTRACTORS RECOMMENDATIONS.

ZINCALUME BARGE CAPPING.

9MM THICK COMPRESSED FIBRE CEMENT SHEET FASCIA SCREW FIXED TO 75x38 GALV. TOP HAT SECTIONS AT 600 CTS. MAX. NOTE: TAPE BEHIND VERTICAL JOINTS WITH 50 MM WIDE UNISIL TAPE. GASKET.

15 MM THICK BLUESTONE FACING EPOXY / PIN TO IN-SITU CONC. WALL.

10 MM THICK P/BOARD ON FURRING CHANNELS. PROVIDE STEEL GIRT BETWEEN OUTRIGGER ARM WHERE REQUIRED.

RETURN AWNING FABRIC TO FASCIA. FIX DOWN WITH S/STEEL ALL THREAD BOLTED BACK TO 100 x 100 RA TRIMMER. GAP OFF AWNING FROM FASCIA WITH S/STEEL SPACER & ACORN NUT TO LOCATE BOTTOM OF AWNING INTO GUTTER.

WINDOW HEAD. 2450 AFL.

60 X 4·2 MM WESTERN RED CEDAR INTERNAL VENETIAN BLINDS. REFER FINISHES SCHEDULE.

NOTE: GUTTER TO BE FIXED LEVEL WITH HEAD OF WINDOW (NO FALL) GUTTER FIXING BRACKETS TO MATCH PAINT FINISH & COLOUR OF GUTTER.

7

4 *Detail of removable pin*
5 *Detail of roof support and wall junction*
6 *View from Southbank promenade*
7 *Section through wall/ceiling junction*

8

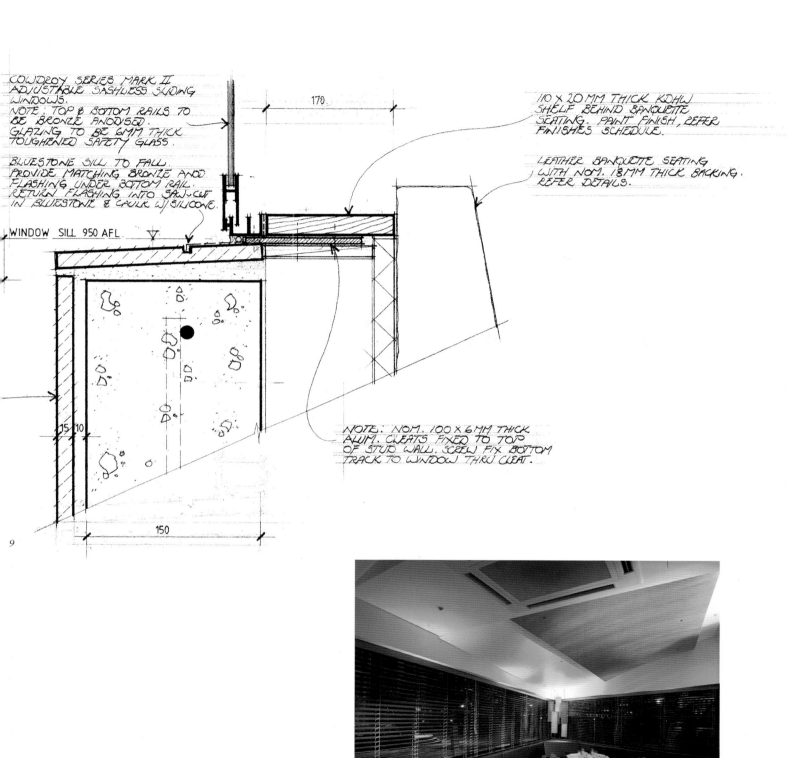

COWDROY SERIES MARK II
ADJUSTABLE SASHLESS SLIDING
WINDOWS.
NOTE: TOP & BOTTOM RAILS TO
BE BRONZE ANODISED.
GLAZING TO BE 6MM THICK
TOUGHENED SAFETY GLASS.

BLUESTONE SILL TO FALL.
PROVIDE MATCHING BRONZE ANOD
FLASHING UNDER BOTTOM RAIL.
RETURN FLASHING INTO SAW-CUT
IN BLUESTONE & CAULK W/ SILICONE.

WINDOW SILL 950 AFL

170

110 x 20 MM THICK KDHW
SHELF BEHIND BANQUETTE
SEATING. PAINT FINISH, REFER
FINISHES SCHEDULE.

LEATHER BANQUETTE SEATING
WITH NOM. 18MM THICK BACKING.
REFER DETAILS.

NOTE: NOM. 100 x 6 MM THICK
ALUM. CLEATS FIXED TO TOP
OF STUD WALL. SCREW FIX BOTTOM
TRACK TO WINDOW THRU CLEAT.

15 10

150

9

8&10   *Function room*
   9   *Sill detail at base wall*
Photography: Blain Crellin

10

TOWER AND OBSERVATION DECK

THE POINT, ALBERT PARK LAKE, MELBOURNE, AUSTRALIA
Maddison Architects Pty Ltd

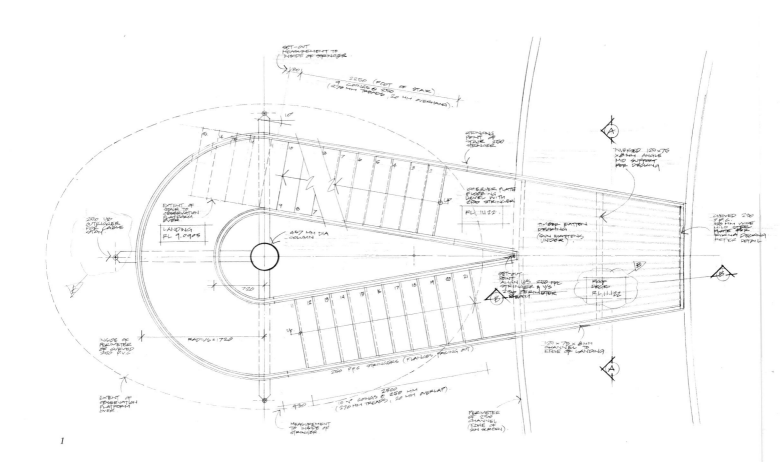

1

2

The Point is a two-storey mixed-use building situated by Albert Park Lake in Melbourne, Australia. The ground floor contains a café, kitchen, kiosk, boat hire, services and an open-plan office for the organisation that manages the park. Upstairs is a formal restaurant, kitchen, function room, office and services. An 11-metre-high observation tower is also part of the development, which can be accessed by the public.

The design of the building responds directly to an exquisite site on a small promontory. The lake-edge curtainwall façade gently curves with the site topography and opens itself to the sweeping views

across the water and beyond. The city skyline can be glimpsed from the tower and the public areas of the building.

The building has been uncompromisingly modern from the initial sketches; expressed structure wrapped in a glass skin. In terms of its aspirations, the building has responded to its context by forming an obvious exclamation mark at the end of a row of boatsheds. Constructed from stainless and mild steel, the tower is a key element in this composition and provides the necessary drama for its prominent location.

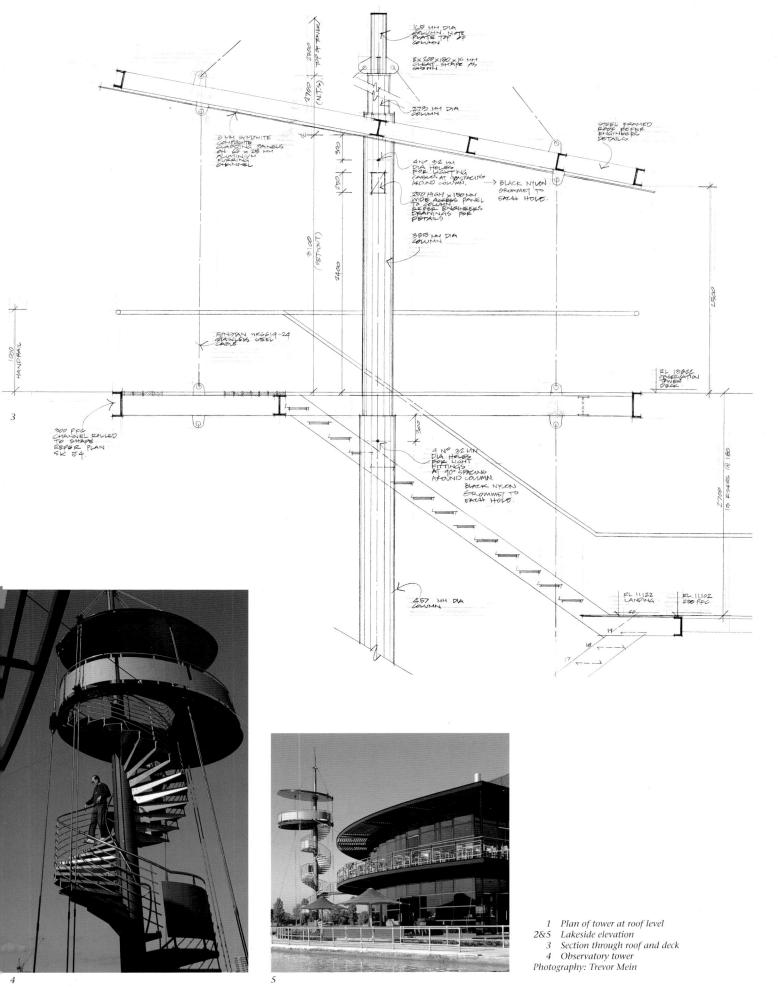

1   Plan of tower at roof level
2&5 Lakeside elevation
3   Section through roof and deck
4   Observatory tower
Photography: Trevor Mein

WALL, STAIR AND BANNISTER

SOUTH YARRA, VICTORIA, AUSTRALIA
Maddison Architects Pty Ltd

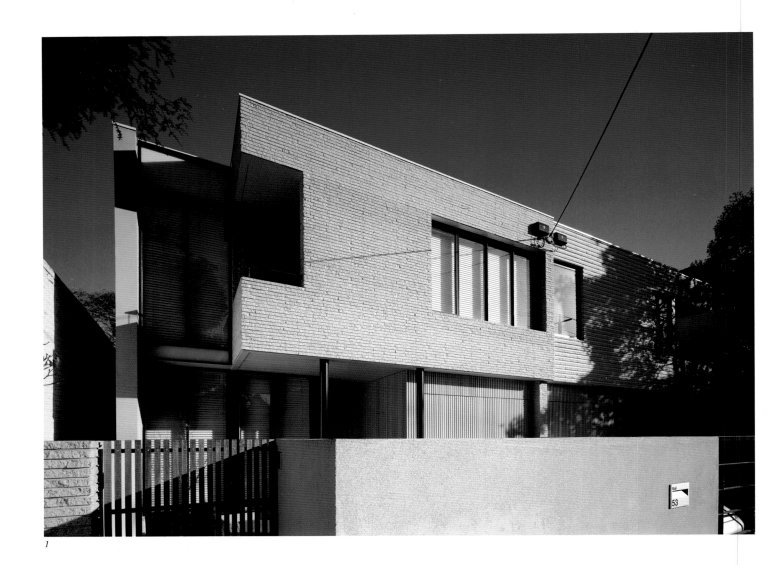

1

This project represents a typical dual-occupancy development within the inner urban zone of Melbourne, Australia and was an opportunity for Maddison Architects to pursue the idea of treating the façade as a continuous whole whilst providing subtle individuality for each housing unit.

The façade is a critical element in this project because of the other elevations which have been built to the edge of the site. The investigation centred on providing a cohesive building that was 'held' together by a skin of split-faced paving blocks.

The composition of the blocks was carefully manipulated to create colour and texture variations in the surface of the façade. The façade cantilevers at the upper level with the window plane breaking loose from the masonry so as to create outdoor decks. Windows have been detailed so that they read as cut-outs in the fabric of masonry.

At the lower level, a taut surface of vertical battens conceals a garage and proceeds through the entry to wrap the interior.

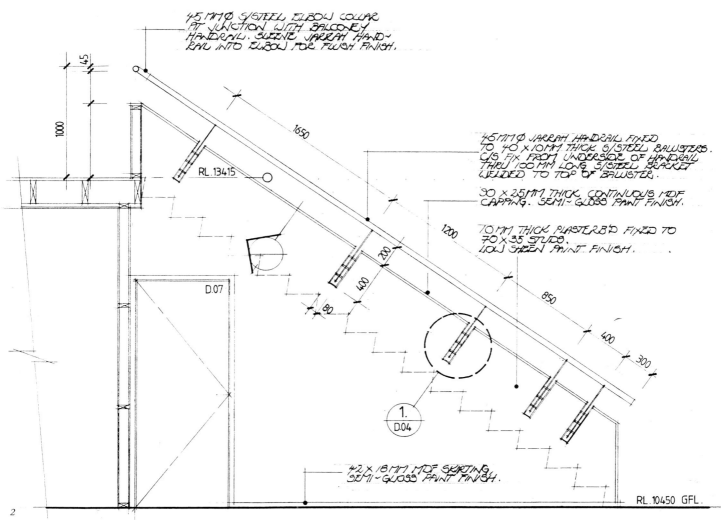

45 MM Ø S/STEEL ELBOW COLLAR
AT JUNCTION WITH BALCONEY
HANDRAIL. SLEEVE JARRAH HAND-
RAIL INTO ELBOW FOR FLUSH FINISH.

45 MM Ø JARRAH HANDRAIL FIXED
TO 40 x 10 MM THICK S/STEEL BALUSTERS.
C/S FIX FROM UNDERSIDE OF HANDRAIL
THRU 100 MM LONG S/STEEL BRACKET
WELDED TO TOP OF BALUSTER.

90 x 25 MM THICK CONTINUOUS MDF
CAPPING. SEMI-GLOSS PAINT FINISH.

70 MM THICK PLASTERB'D FIXED TO
70 x 35 STUDS.
LOW SHEEN PAINT FINISH.

45

1000

1650

RL.13415

200

400

80

1200

850

400

300

D.07

1.
D.04

42 x 18 MM MDF SKIRTING.
SEMI-GLOSS PAINT FINISH.

RL.10450 GFL.

2

1   Front façade
2   Stair elevation
3   Handrail and bannister

The interior features elements that are highly
wrought and crafted, an example being the stair.
The handrail is separated from the plasterboard
wall, with stainless steel pockets and uprights
spaced at ever increasing centres as one moves
through to the first floor. The reward of the project
comes with the resultant cohesive form, which
overcomes the problems of this restricted site, and
creates a separate identity for both groups of
occupants.

3

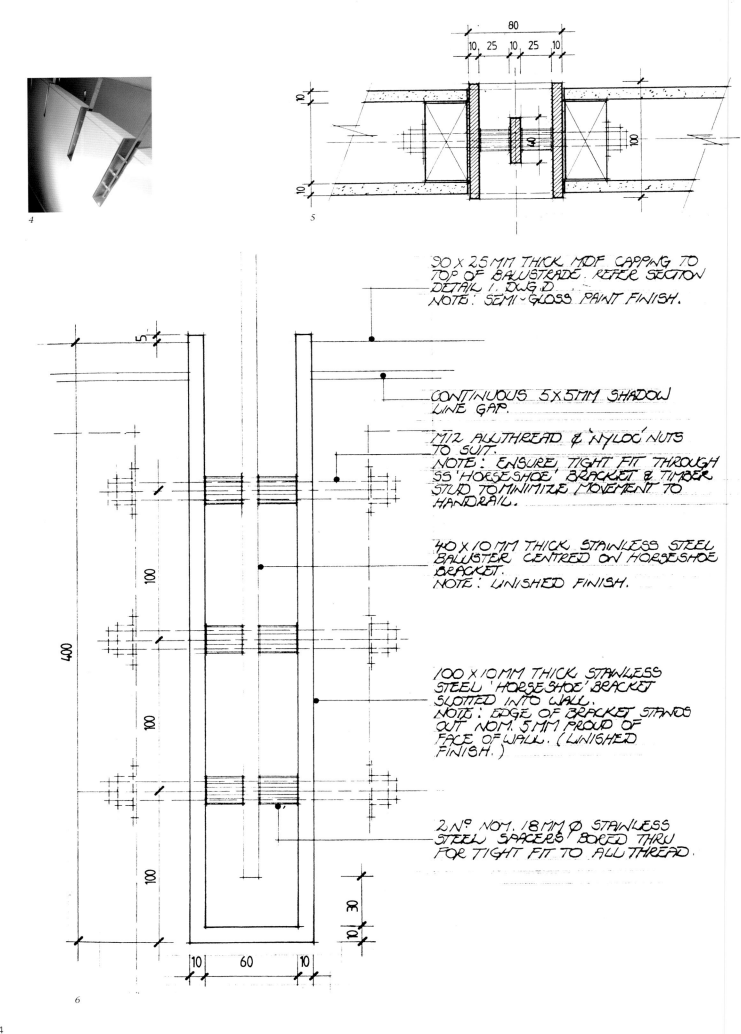

4

5

80

10 25 10 25 10

10

30

100

90 X 25 MM THICK MDF CAPPING TO
TOP OF BALUSTRADE. REFER SECTION
DETAIL 1, DWG D.
NOTE: SEMI-GLOSS PAINT FINISH.

5

CONTINUOUS 5 X 5 MM SHADOW
LINE GAP.

M12 ALLTHREAD & 'NYLOC' NUTS
TO SUIT.
NOTE: ENSURE TIGHT FIT THROUGH
SS 'HORSESHOE' BRACKET & TIMBER
STUD TO MINIMIZE MOVEMENT TO
HANDRAIL.

40 X 10 MM THICK STAINLESS STEEL
BALUSTER CENTRED ON HORSESHOE
BRACKET.
NOTE: LINISHED FINISH.

100 X 10 MM THICK STAINLESS
STEEL 'HORSESHOE' BRACKET
SLOTTED INTO WALL.
NOTE: EDGE OF BRACKET STANDS
OUT NOM. 5 MM PROUD OF
FACE OF WALL. (LINISHED
FINISH.)

2 N° NOM. 18 MM Ø STAINLESS
STEEL SPACERS BORED THRU
FOR TIGHT FIT TO ALLTHREAD.

400

100

100

100

30

10

10

60

10

6

7

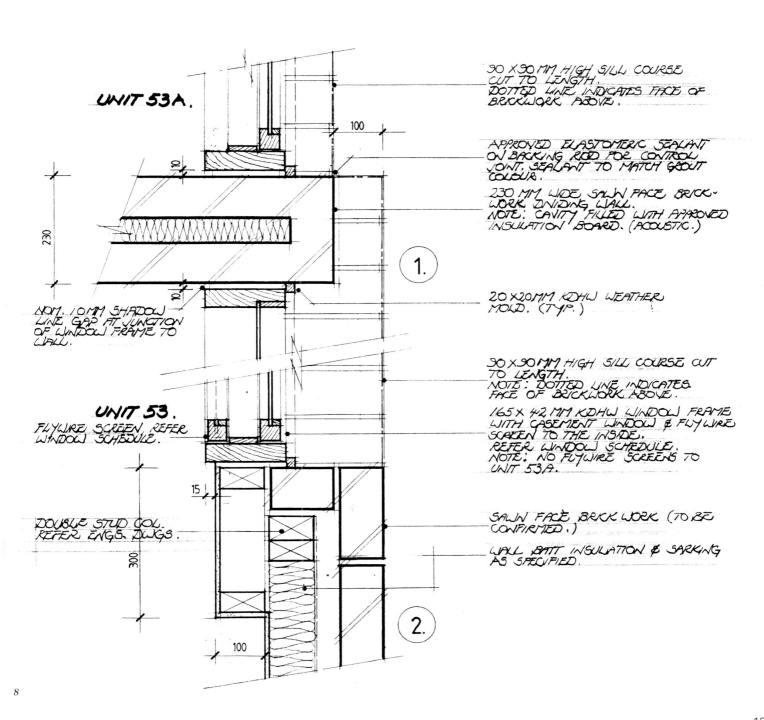

UNIT 53A.

90 X 90 MM HIGH SILL COURSE CUT TO LENGTH.
DOTTED LINE INDICATES FACE OF BRICKWORK ABOVE.

APPROVED ELASTOMERIC SEALANT ON BACKING ROD FOR CONTROL JOINT. SEALANT TO MATCH GROUT COLOUR.

230 MM WIDE SAWN FACE BRICKWORK DIVIDING WALL.
NOTE: CAVITY FILLED WITH APPROVED INSULATION BOARD. (ACOUSTIC.)

1.

20 X 20MM KDHW WEATHER MOLD. (TYP.)

NOM. 10 MM SHADOW LINE GAP AT JUNCTION OF WINDOW FRAME TO WALL.

90 X 90 MM HIGH SILL COURSE CUT TO LENGTH.
NOTE: DOTTED LINE INDICATES FACE OF BRICKWORK ABOVE.

UNIT 53.
FLYWIRE SCREEN REFER WINDOW SCHEDULE.

165 X 42 MM KDHW WINDOW FRAME WITH CASEMENT WINDOW & FLYWIRE SCREEN TO THE INSIDE.
REFER WINDOW SCHEDULE.
NOTE: NO FLYWIRE SCREENS TO UNIT 53A.

DOUBLE STUD COL. REFER ENG'S. DWGS.

SAWN FACE BRICKWORK (TO BE CONFIRMED.)

WALL BATT INSULATION & SARKING AS SPECIFIED.

2.

8

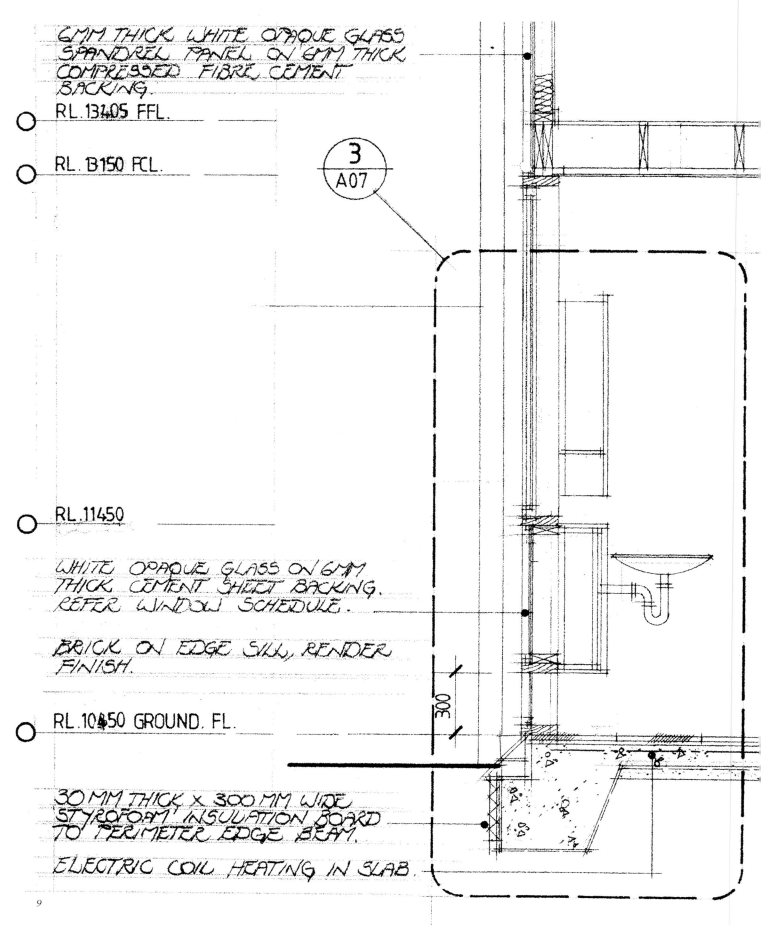

6MM THICK WHITE OPAQUE GLASS
SPANDREL PANEL ON 6MM THICK
COMPRESSED FIBRE CEMENT
BACKING.

RL. 13405 FFL.

RL. 13150 FCL.

③
A07

RL. 11450

WHITE OPAQUE GLASS ON 6MM
THICK CEMENT SHEET BACKING.
REFER WINDOW SCHEDULE.

BRICK ON EDGE SILL, RENDER
FINISH.

RL. 10450 GROUND. FL.

300

30 MM THICK × 300 MM WIDE
'STYROFOAM' INSULATION BOARD
TO PERIMETER EDGE BEAM.

ELECTRIC COIL HEATING IN SLAB.

9

10

SHADING STRUCTURE

ASEA BROWN BOVERI (ABB), ATHENS, GREECE
Meletitiki – Alexandros N. Tombazis & Associates Architects, Ltd

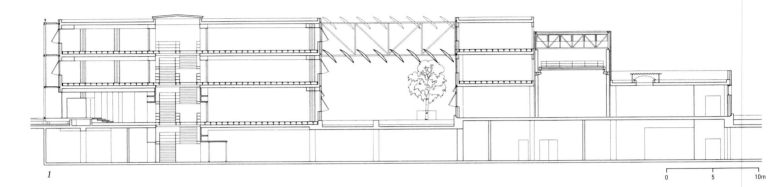

1

0   5   10m

2

3

1   Cross section
2   Atrium shed
3   Shading fins over atrium
4   Section metal frame of I-beam elements
    carries shade
Photography: Dimitris Kalapodas

This 7,000-square-metre complex consists of two buildings. The building towards the highway houses administration facilities, while the other building accommodates a warehouse and hall for assembling electrical components.

The office building, with its trapezoidal shape, has three storeys. The ground floor houses general functions, while the upper two floors accommodate offices. A second steel frame façade has been created near the highway that shades the northwest elevation and gives the building a unique identity. A large shallow reflecting pool enhances this impression.

The assembly building consists of three aisles, the middle one, of great height, is covered by a 'chainsaw-tooth' roof that provides daylight to the other two aisles. The open space between the two buildings is covered by a metal shading structure, the building is clad with aluminium and glazed panels. All office spaces are provided with false ceilings and raised floors.

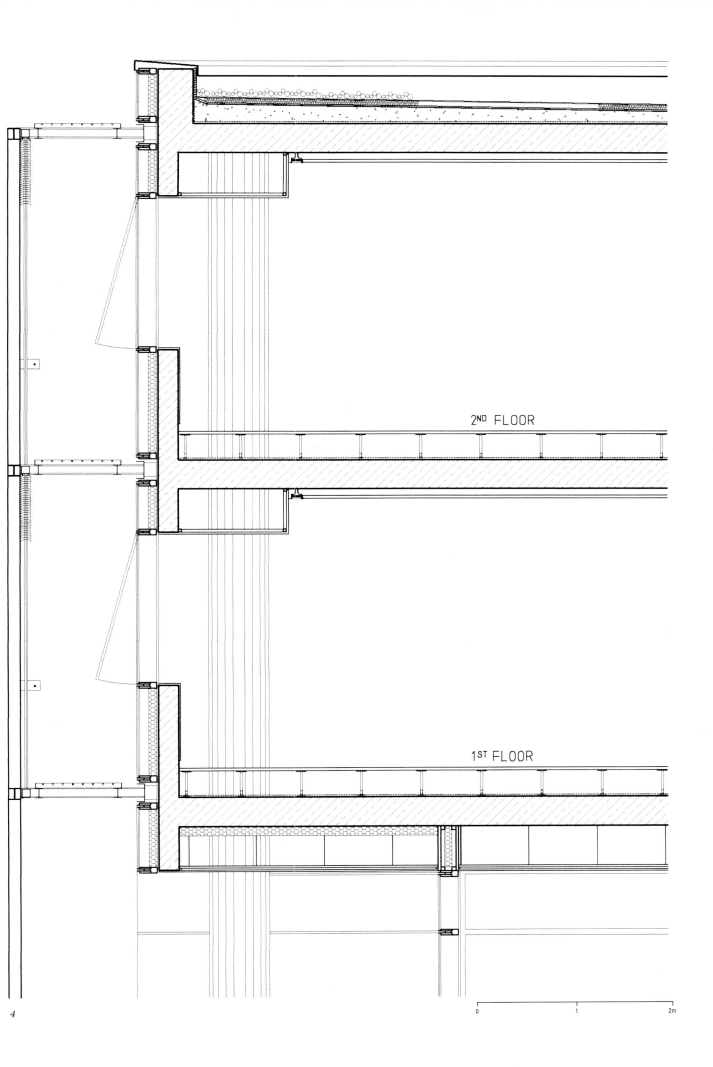

2ND FLOOR

1ST FLOOR

4

0   1   2m

SHADING SYSTEM

GREEK REFINERY HEADQUARTERS, ASPROPYRGOS, GREECE
Meletitiki – Alexandros N. Tombazis and Associates Architects, Ltd

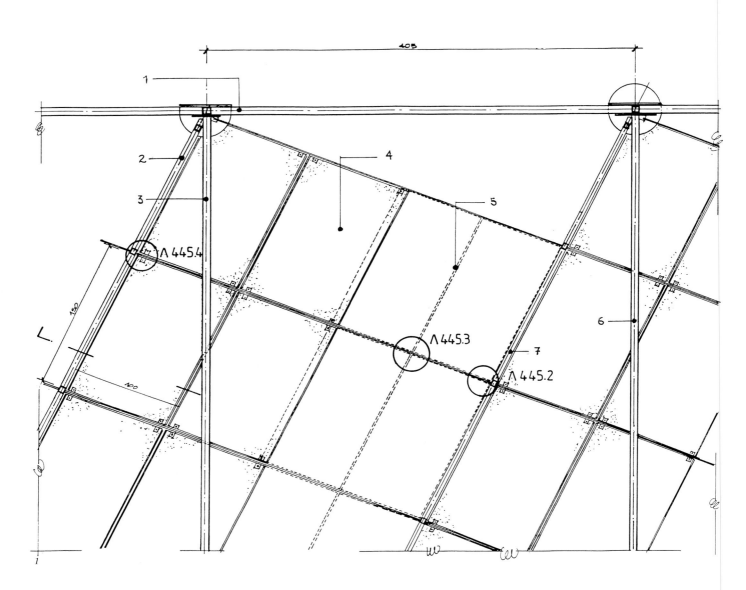

2

The shading devices over the atrium, between the office and the assembly building, are made of fins, which are placed along the northwest axis and supported by 14-metre-long metal frame beams that bridge the span between the buildings every eight metres.

The fins are made of perforated metal sheet bent on bow-like frames installed centrally across eight-metre-long tubular axes. A second elevation has been created along the northwest façade of the building. A metal frame made of I-beam elements carries the shading device and also supports a metal grill corridor for cleaning and maintenance of the façade.

The shading system consists of retractable revolving aluminium louvres, controlled by the central building management system. The shading fins comprise perforated metal panels hung with tension wires from a 'network' of metal poles and frame beams. The louvres are made of laminated glass panels with a silkscreen-printed internal surface, providing a shading coefficient of 70 per cent.

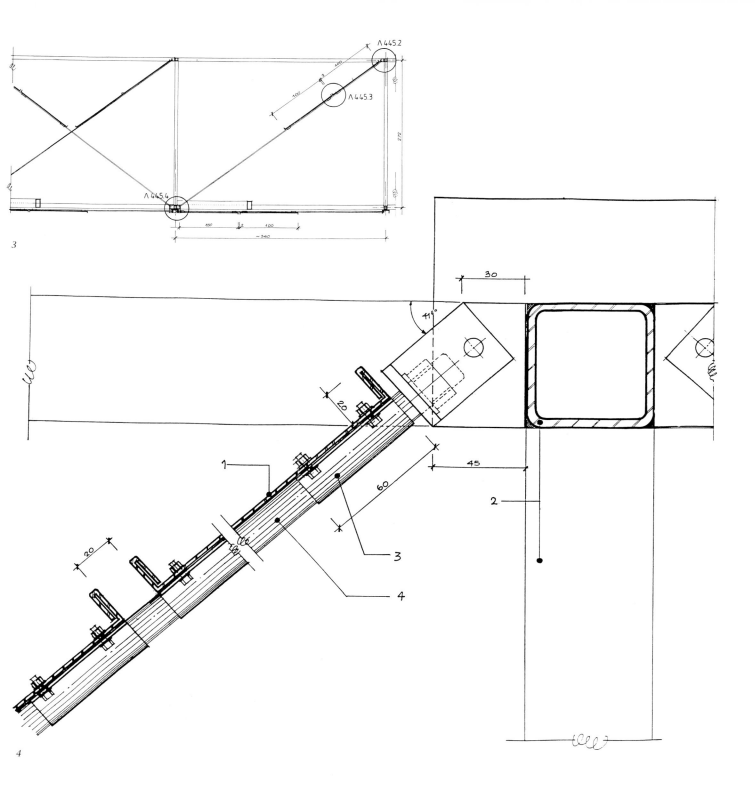

3

4

Λ445.2

Λ445.3

Λ445.4

41°

1

2

3

4

20

20

60

45

30

~360

100   100

5

6

1   Plan of metal frame
2,5&6 Shading fins and network of metal
       poles and frame beams
3   Plan of shading fin
4   Detail of hinge
Photography: Nikos Danielidis

VERTICAL GLASS PANELS

AVAX S.A. HEADQUARTERS, ATHENS, GREECE
Meletitiki – Alexandros N. Tombazis & Associates Architects, Ltd

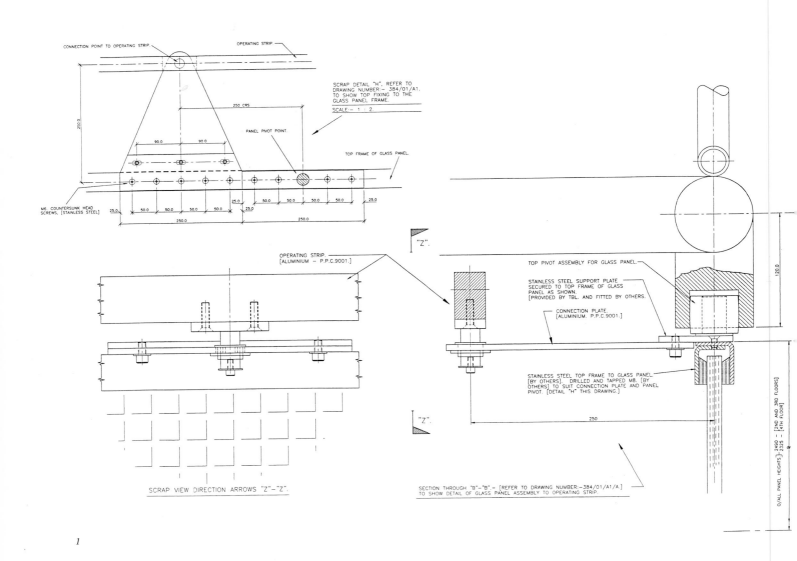

1

1 Moveable glass panels detail
2 Shading glass panels in closed position
3 Shading glass panels in open position
4 Plan view of glass panels in 45 degree open
   position
Photography: Nikos Danielidis

This building, housing the headquarters of 'AVAX' S.A., a major contracting company, is situated in downtown Athens, Greece on the east-facing slope of Lycabettus Hill. It comprises three basement levels, and six levels above ground totalling 3,050 square metres. The main aim of the design was to apply bioclimatic features to limit the energy demands and create a comfortable environment.

The structural frame is a combination of waffle-reinforced concrete slabs and sheer walls and a steel structure with raised floors. The main façade consists of vertical glass panels. Bioclimatic features have been incorporated in the design,

including special vertical glass louvres shading the east façade which consists of laminated glass panels with silk screen-printed internal surfaces (shading co-efficient of 70 per cent). They rotate around a vertical axis in response to solar movement.

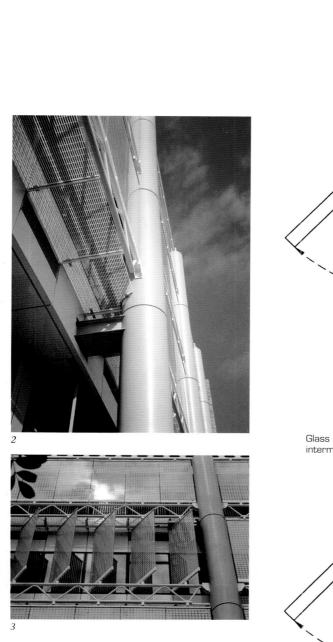

2

3

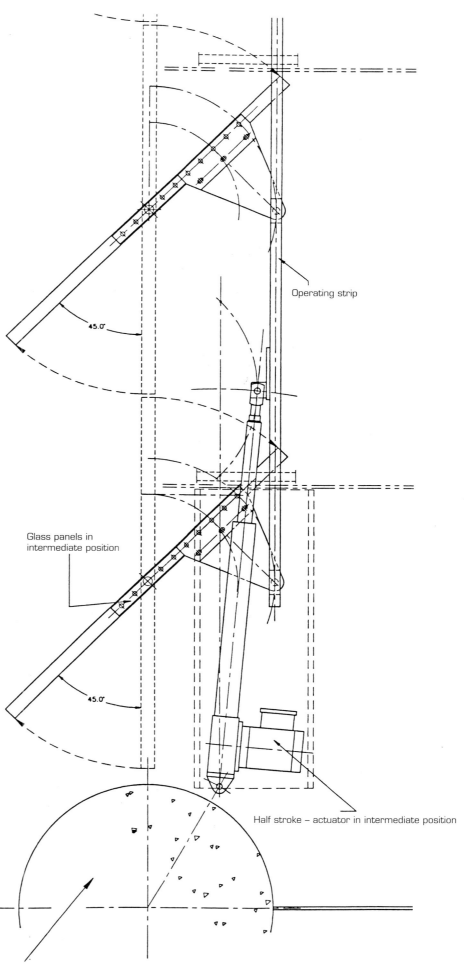

Operating strip

45.0°

Glass panels in
intermediate position

45.0°

Half stroke – actuator in intermediate position

4

143

LABORATORY WORKSPACE

THE WHITNEY PAVILION, WEILL MEDICAL COLLEGE, CORNELL UNIVERSITY, NEW YORK, NEW YORK, USA
Mitchell/Giurgola Architects, LLP

1

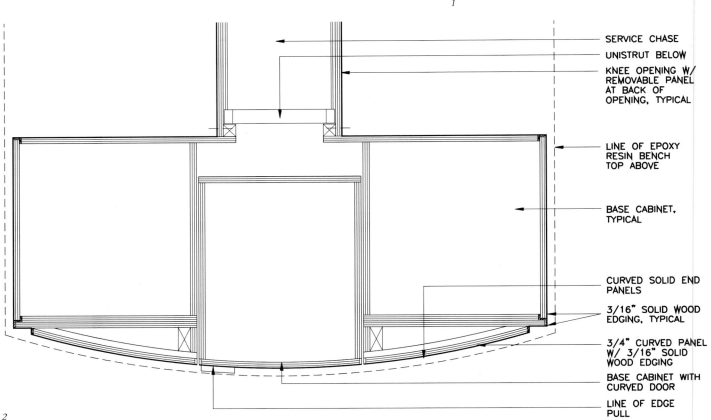

SERVICE CHASE

UNISTRUT BELOW

KNEE OPENING W/
REMOVABLE PANEL
AT BACK OF
OPENING, TYPICAL

LINE OF EPOXY
RESIN BENCH
TOP ABOVE

BASE CABINET,
TYPICAL

CURVED SOLID END
PANELS

3/16" SOLID WOOD
EDGING, TYPICAL

3/4" CURVED PANEL
W/ 3/16" SOLID
WOOD EDGING

BASE CABINET WITH
CURVED DOOR

LINE OF EDGE
PULL

2

1 Open laboratory
2 Lab plan detail
3 Laboratory bench
4 Lab bench elevation
Photography: Jeff Goldberg/Esto

The Whitney Pavilion is a recently renovated 4645-square-metre, 1930s-era complex of outdated patient care spaces redesigned to accommodate new research laboratories for the study of genetic medicine, structural biology and neuroscience.

Each of the seven laboratory floors is designed with the same basic configuration: a racetrack with shared support functions in the centre and primary circulation at the perimeter of two open lab precincts.

Taking advantage of natural light through a perimeter arrangement, the laboratory space is open and continuous. In these large open spaces,

bench areas can easily be adjusted for individual researchers with minimal disruption. While the configuration of drawers and outlets can be customised for each bench, the overall profile is constant, incorporating a curved edge that provides additional table space.

The laboratory floors are interconnected through the creation of a new stair that acts as a vibrant vertical link. The stair is brought into the labs themselves through the use of translucent fireproof glass walls. The aesthetic of the laboratory extends into the stair through the use of maple railings, slate and natural light.

3

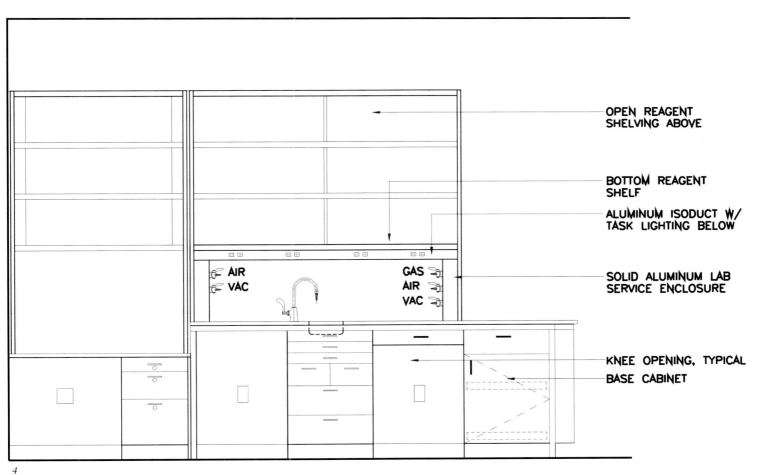

OPEN REAGENT
SHELVING ABOVE

BOTTOM REAGENT
SHELF

ALUMINUM ISODUCT W/
TASK LIGHTING BELOW

SOLID ALUMINUM LAB
SERVICE ENCLOSURE

KNEE OPENING, TYPICAL

BASE CABINET

AIR
VAC

GAS
AIR
VAC

4

ROOF

SONY CENTER, BERLIN, GERMANY
Murphy/Jahn Inc Architects

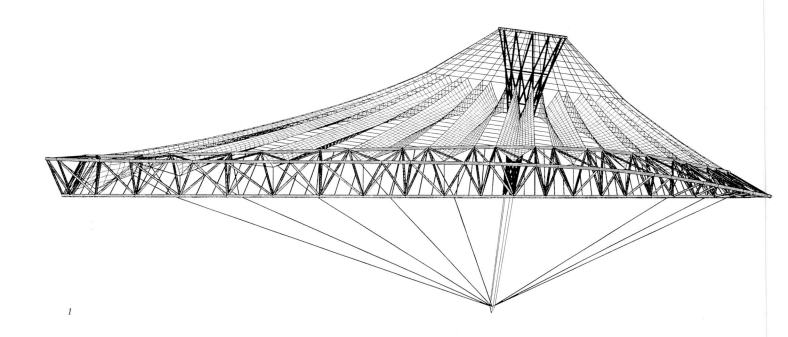

1

The roof of the Sony Center in Berlin is an elliptical structure providing shading and protection from the elements. It is a heroic display of the latest state-of-the-art cable, membrane and glass technology. One third of the roof is glazed, assuring a view to the outside, ecological and economical construction and desired contrast and interesting lighting. The result is a cable-reinforced fibreglass membrane insuring transparency, lightweight, long life and economy.

The roof is a membrane stressed between an inner tension ring and an outer compression ring and gaining-profile via the inclined king post. The two cable families have been stressed against one another to provide the surface with a tautness to hold form and support load. The upper cables serve the primary function of carrying gravity load, principally snow load. In turn, the lower cable set resist the uplift force caused by wind load on the lightweight structure.

The roof contains a significant area of glass and the need to control displacements to safeguard this brittle material is a prime design consideration. In addition, an approach is in place at the detailing level to create the glass strips as individual articulated framed units capable of

2

3

1 Elevation of roof structure
2 External view of roof and curtainwall at night
3 Interior view of roof and commercial façade

relatively large movements. This has been achieved via a lapping process possible in a non-sealed covering.

Due to the relative flatness of the profile, the primary cables generate large tension forces that are in turn resisted by the ring beam. The steel ring beam has been typically supported at 12-metre spacing by columns of the adjacent buildings. In turn, the king post base is supported by six inclined ties whose horizontal and vertical trusts are anchored to the adjacent building, minimising bending action in the ring beam.

4

4&5   *Interior view of roof*
6   *Roof detail*
Photography: Henkelmann (2,3), Sony/P. Adenis (4,5)

5

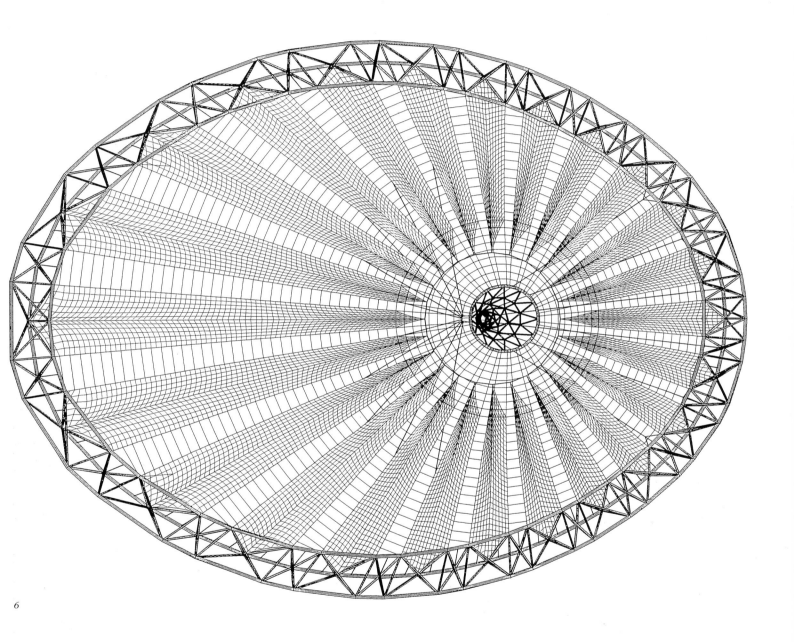

6

HOTEL WITH TRADITIONAL DETAILS

SHERATON SUZHOU HOTEL, SUZHOU, PEOPLES REPUBLIC OF CHINA
P&T Group

1

1   *Reception pavilion from garden*
2   *Exposed roof structure of reception pavilion*
3   *Plan of reception pavilion reflective ceiling*
4   *Ramp to reception*
5   *Elevation of ramp to reception*

Located in the historic centre of Suzhou, the hotel has been designed to complement adjoining historic monuments, such as the 1,800-year-old ruins of the Suzhou City Wall and the 247 AD 'Puiguang Ta' Pagoda.

The five-star hotel provides 400 rooms and associated facilities in a distinct architectural setting. Guestrooms have been provided along an artificial canal and several courtyards, which have been landscaped in the traditional manner.

All public and back-of-house facilities have been located in a reinterpreted city wall structure, accessed via ramps and topped with Suzhou Chinese style pavilions, which house the main lobby, restaurants and executive accommodation. Finished in local materials, local granite and roof tiles, the hotel provides a culturally appropriate addition to the historic setting.

2

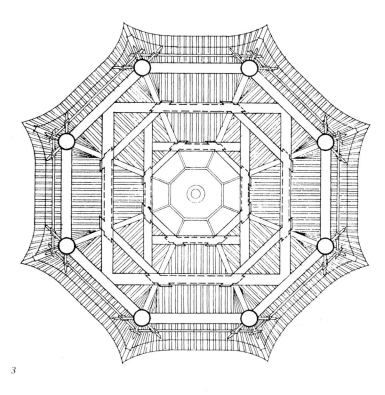

3

4

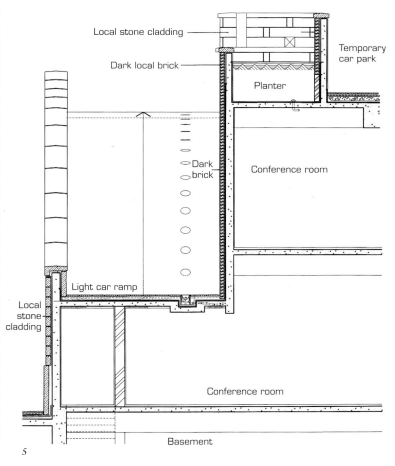

Local stone cladding

Dark local brick

Temporary car park

Planter

Dark brick

Conference room

Light car ramp

Local stone cladding

Conference room

Basement

5

6

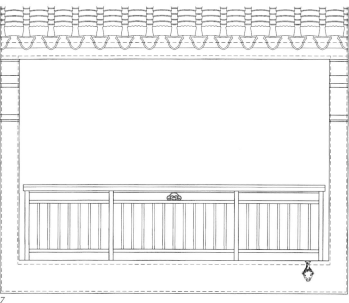

7

6   *Octagonal reception pavilion sitting on the*
     reinterpreted city wall structure
7   *Elevation of balcony*
8   *Typical guest room balcony*
9   *Section detail of guestroom balcony*

8

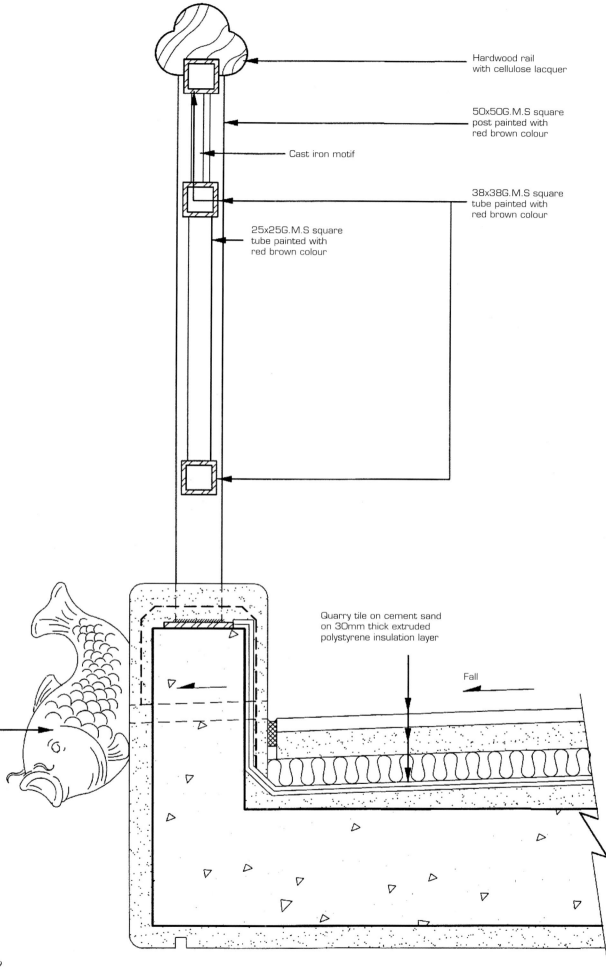

Hardwood rail
with cellulose lacquer

50x50G.M.S square
post painted with
red brown colour

Cast iron motif

38x38G.M.S square
tube painted with
red brown colour

25x25G.M.S square
tube painted with
red brown colour

Quarry tile on cement sand
on 30mm thick extruded
polystyrene insulation layer

Fall

9

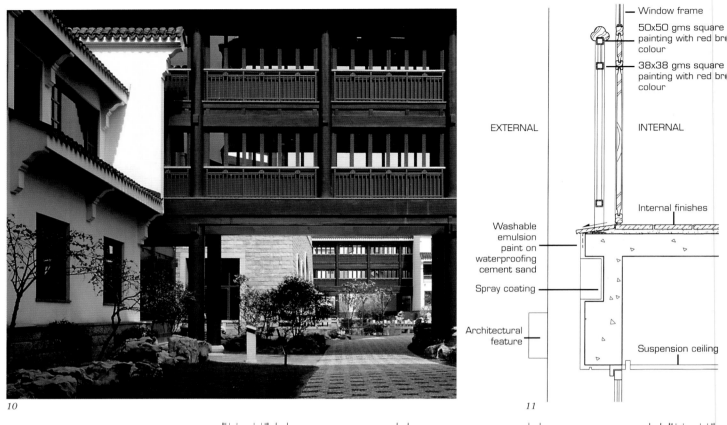

10

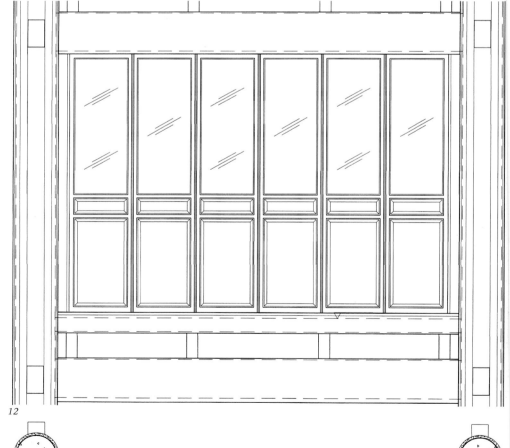

11

Window frame

50x50 gms square
painting with red bro
colour

38x38 gms square
painting with red bro
colour

EXTERNAL

INTERNAL

Internal finishes

Washable
emulsion
paint on
waterproofing
cement sand

Spray coating

Architectural
feature

Suspension ceiling

12

13

10 Timber shutters along corridor
11 Section of timber shutters along corridor
12 Elevation of timber shutters along
    corridor
13 Plan of timber shutters along corridor
14 Elevation of arched opening
15 Section of arch
16 Arched opening between indoor and
    outdoor pool recalling traditional water
    gate
Photography: Kerum Ip

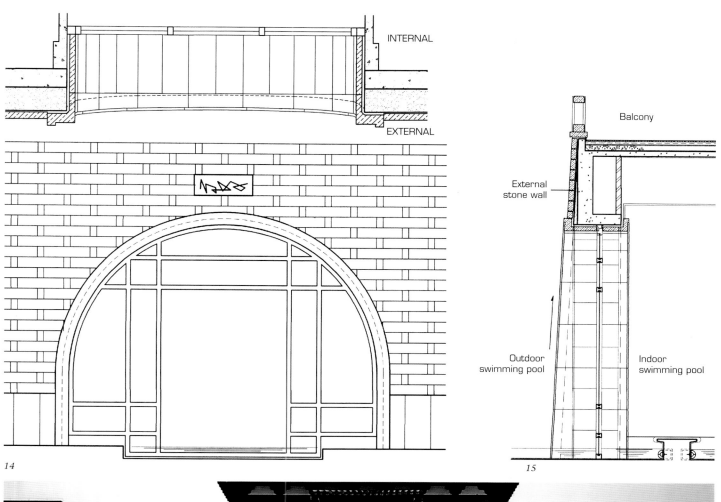

INTERNAL

EXTERNAL

Balcony

External
stone wall

Outdoor
swimming pool

Indoor
swimming pool

14

15

16

CEILINGS, WALLS AND SUNSHADES

BIBLIOTÈQUE NATIONALE DE FRANCE, PARIS, FRANCE
Dominique Perrault Architecte

1

The Bibliotèque Nationale De France has met various criteria to establish itself as a great building. It has been depicted as a place, not a building, both a square for Paris and a library for France, a symbolic place, a magic place and an urban place.

It has been built on a stretch of industrial wasteland on the banks of the Seine in the east end of Paris and while enormous in size, is not ostentatious. The enormous building has proposed to the history of France a focus on immateriality and non-ostentation. This context has engendered the concept of the project.

The four corner towers of the design resemble four open books, all facing one another and defining a symbolic place. This project is a piece of art, a minimalist installation in which 'less is more' emotion. The towers have a double skin and sun filters that multiply the reflections and magnify the shadows.

A diaphanous light rises up through the interior of the glass towers, culminating in the four topmost points, which shimmer like four lighthouse beacons. This liquid light spreads over the square, while the towers are reflected on the surface of the Seine.

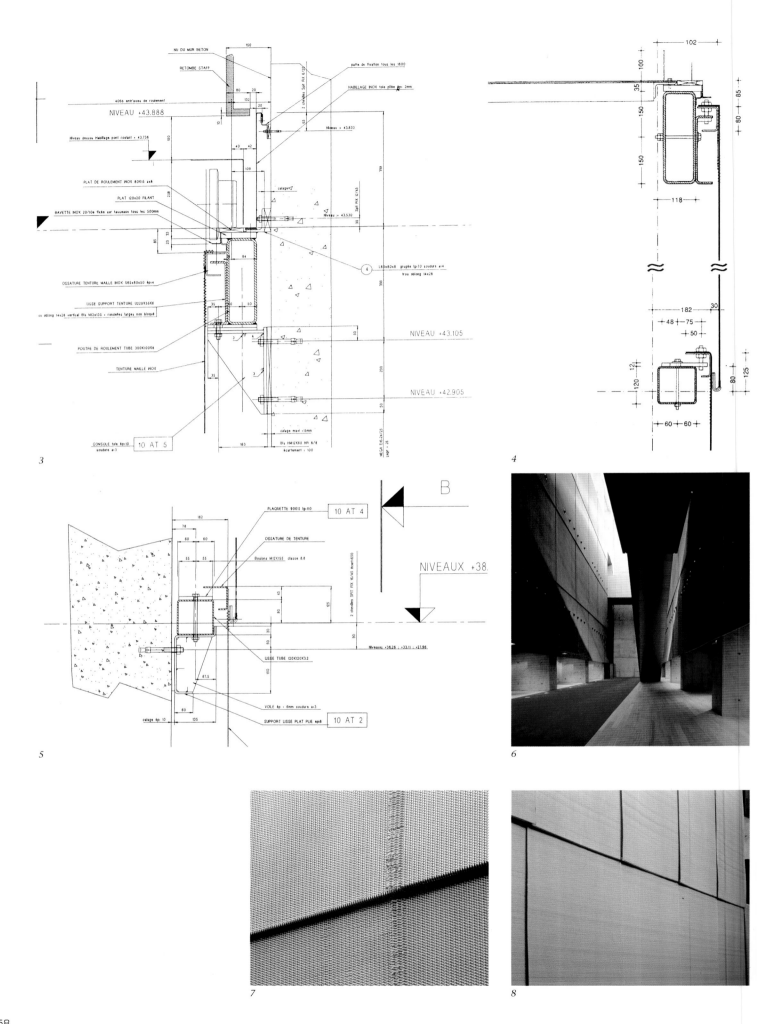

3

NU DU MUR BETON

RETOMBE STAFF

NIVEAU +43.888

406b entr'axes de roulement

Niveau dessus Habillage pont roulant + 43.738

PLAT DE ROULEMENT INOX 80X15 4x8

PLAT I20x20 FILANT

BAVETTE INOX 20/10e fixée sur tasseaux tous les 500mm

OSSATURE TENTURE MAILLE INOX U65x80x50 ép:4

LISSE SUPPORT TENTURE U220X55X6

ou oblong 14x28 vertical B4 M12x135 + rondelles larges non bloquée

POUTRE DE ROULEMENT TUBE 300X100X8

TENTURE MAILLE INOX

CONSOLE tole ép:10
soudure a:3

10 AT 5

patte de fixation tous les 1800

HABILLAGE INOX tole pliée ép: 2mm

Niveau + 43.833

calage

Niveau + 43.530

L80x60x8 grugée lg:70 soudure a:4
trou oblong 14x28

NIVEAU +43.105

NIVEAU +42.905

calage maxi <16mm

B4 HM12X60 HR 8/8
écartement = 100

4

102

100

35

118

182 30
48 75
50

120 12

60 60

5

B

PLAQUETTE 90X12 lg:110

10 AT 4

OSSATURE DE TENTURE

Boulons M12X155 classe 8.8

NIVEAUX +38.

LISSE TUBE 120X120X3.2

VOILE ép : 6mm soudure a:3

SUPPORT LISSE PLAT PLIE ép:8

10 AT 2

Niveaux +38.26 ; +33.11 ; +27.96

6

7

8

158

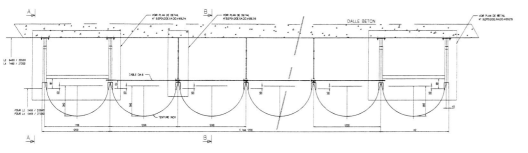

COUPE A-A SUR CONTREVENTEMENT

COUPE B-B SUR TENTURE INOX COURANTE

9

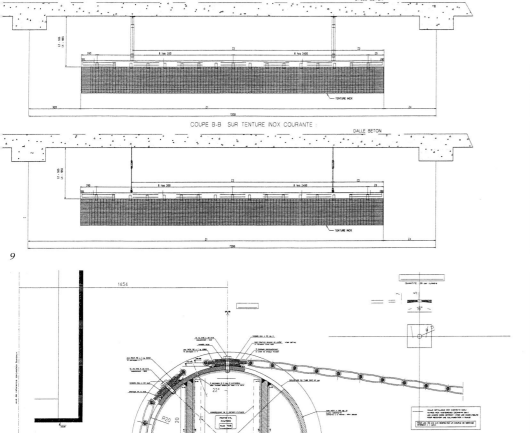

10

11

12

Architectural wire mesh panels cover the bare concrete walls of the entrance halls of the research reading rooms. The 600 stainless steel elements cover the overall room height of 30 metres and are based on traditional Gobelins.

The stainless steel wire mesh hangs like 'flowing cloth' in wide, even arches under the ceiling. A substructure of H-shaped profiles has been fastened to the ceiling and the meshed panels suspended by hanging mesh.

Flat, stretched, cassette-like panels form the ceilings in other rooms of the library. For this purpose, the warp cables of the wire mesh have been compressed into loops along the edges. A round bar made from stainless steel is threaded through these loops. So-called gripper arms have been attached to the substructure of the ceiling to hold the round bars and keep the wire mesh stretched and positioned properly.

13

159

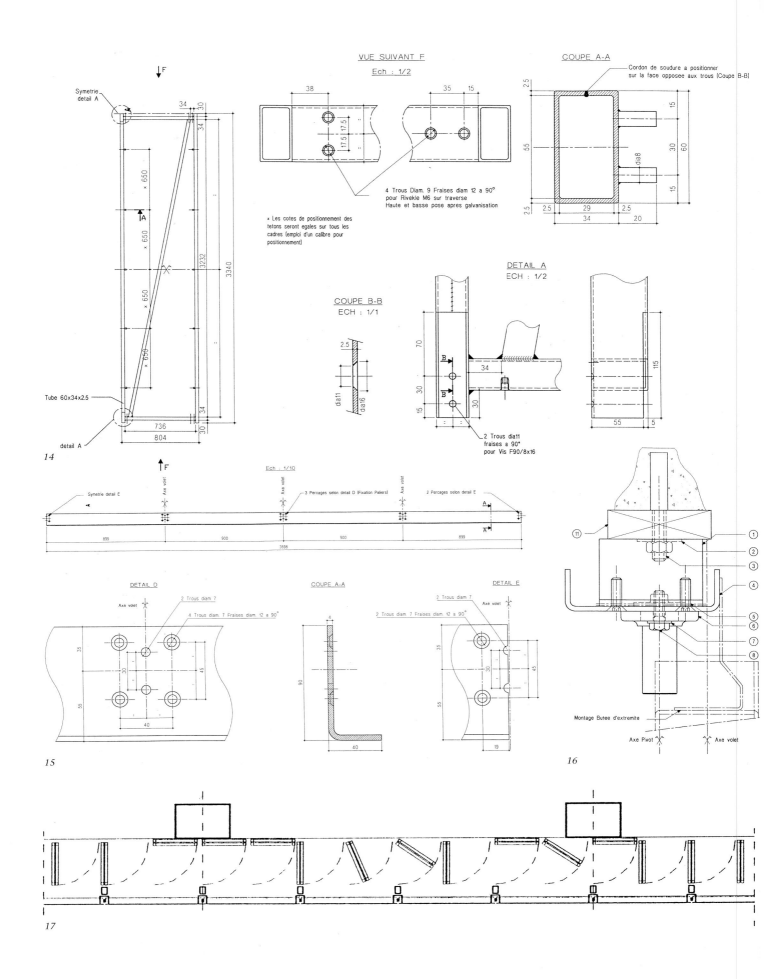

VUE SUIVANT F
Ech : 1/2

COUPE A-A

Cordon de soudure a positionner
sur la face opposee aux trous (Coupe B-B)

4 Trous Diam. 9 Fraises diam 12 a 90°
pour Rivekle M6 sur traverse
Haute et basse pose apres galvanisation

x Les cotes de positionnement des
tetons seront egales sur tous les
cadres (emploi d'un calibre pour
positionnement)

DETAIL A
ECH : 1/2

COUPE B-B
ECH : 1/1

2 Trous dia11
fraises a 90°
pour Vis F90/8x16

Symetrie
detail A

Tube 60x34x2.5

detail A

14

Symetrie detail E

Axe volet

Ech : 1/10

Axe volet

3 Percages selon detail D (Fixation Paliers)

Axe volet

2 Percages selon detail E

DETAIL D

2 Trous diam 7

4 Trous diam. 7 Fraises diam. 12 a 90°

Axe volet

COUPE A-A

DETAIL E

2 Trous diam 7

2 Trous diam. 7 Fraises diam. 12 a 90°

Axe volet

Montage Butee d'extremite

Axe Pivot   Axe volet

15

16

17

160

18

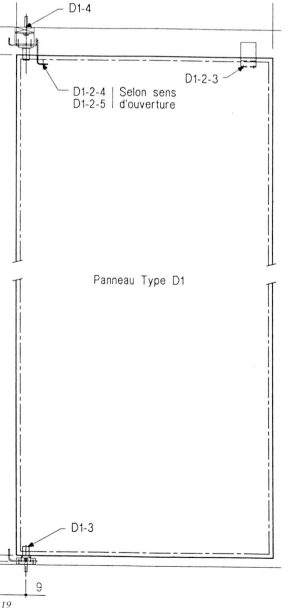

D1-4

D1-2-3

D1-2-4 | Selon sens
D1-2-5 | d'ouverture

Panneau Type D1

D1-3

9

19

20

14,16,19   *Detail of shade*
15   *Wall attachment detail*
17   *Plan of shades*
18&20   *View of curtainwall*
*Photography: Georges Fessy, Michel Denance,
ADAGP*

FACADE

APLIX FACTORY, NANTES METROPOLITAN AREA, FRANCE
Dominique Perrault Architecte

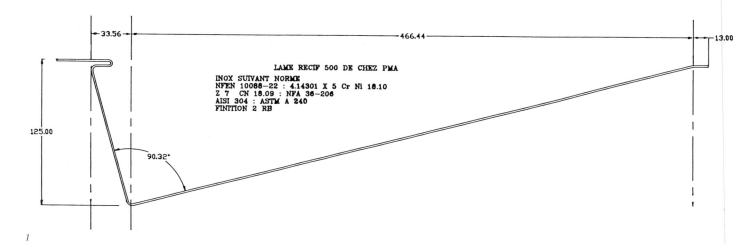

LAME RECIF 500 DE CHEZ PMA
INOX SUIVANT NORME
NFEN 10088-22 : 4.14301 X 5 Cr Ni 18.10
Z 7 CN 18.09 : NFA 36-206
AISI 304 : ASTM A 240
FINITION 2 RB

1

2

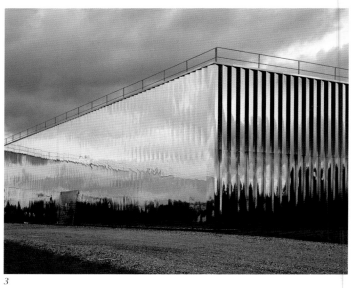

3

1   Detail of the façade module
    designed by Dominique Perrault
2,3,4&6   External view of façade
5   Horizontal section of corner
7   Vertical section
Photography: ADAGP and Georges Fessy

This factory has been built for non-polluting manufacturing, offering a boon to the local jobs market, and lending a certain dynamic to the region. The design has also attempted to offer optimum working conditions and guarantee the flexible integration of future extensions.

The orthogonal site has been covered with a 20 x 20-metre grid, which forms a checkerboard of surfaces. The factory has been composed by the juxtaposition of several 20 x 20-metre blocks, each 7.7 metres high.

The main façade looks onto the main road. Windowless, it expresses a desire for the interiorisation, linked to the architectural project and to the confidentiality of the activity of production.

The structure runs parallel to the main road, and has a continuous and fluid interior space which is the backbone of the building. It allows for the circulation of forklift trucks and the intersection of the entire flow of raw materials and finished product. The interior features three gardens of 20 x 40 metres with lofty russet bark and the bluish foliage of pine trees which will be 12-metres high by the end of construction work.

4

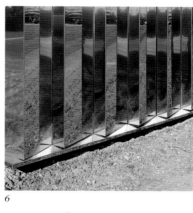

6

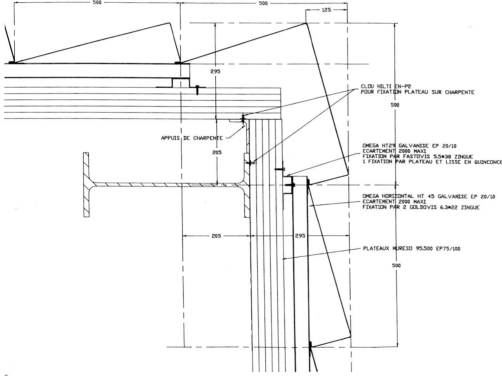

CLOU HILTI EN-P2
POUR FIXATION PLATEAU SUR CHARPENTE

APPUIS DE CHARPENTE

OMEGA HT29 GALVANISE EP 20/10
ECARTEMENT 2000 MAXI
FIXATION PAR FASTOVIS 5.5*38 ZINGUE
1 FIXATION PAR PLATEAU ET LISSE EN QUINCONCE

OMEGA HORIZONTAL HT 45 GALVANISE EP 20/10
ECARTEMENT 2000 MAXI
FIXATION PAR 2 GOLDOVIS 6.3*22 ZINGUE

PLATEAUX MURESO 95.500 EP75/100

5

The structure features slightly burnished metal sheeting, which reflects and blends with the surrounding environment. The design can also be redeveloped to include extensions to the workshop and the addition of parking areas. Extension would be possible with the addition of supplementary squares, creating visual irregularities, especially of the front façade. No extensions to the configuration are envisaged at the moment.

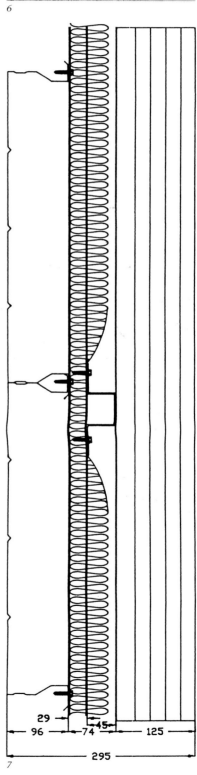

7

GLAZED ROOF

HELSINKI RAILWAY STATION, HELSINKI, FINLAND
Esa Piironen Architects

1

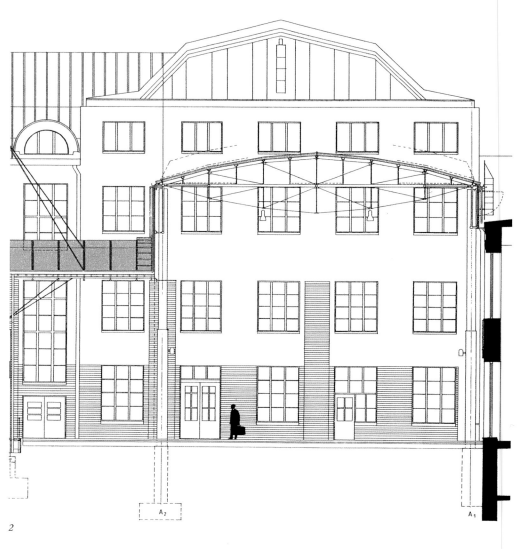

2

1 *End platform shelter without glass*
2 *Section at end platform area*
3 *Cross section*
4 *Detail of roof connection to glass wall*
5 *Tall platform shelter starts at end of
   platform area*
Photography: Jussi Tiainen

The construction of the Helsinki Railway Station was completed in 1919 by Eliel Saarinen, minus a roof over the platforms. Construction work on the first stage–to build a roof – was completed in time for the 450th birthday celebrations of Helsinki, and was needed to cater to the needs of the expected influx of visitors.

The dimensions of the platform shelter were dependent on the existing station building, with a 16 x 69-square-metre end platform shelter over the main platform area in the south adjoining the station hall. The north wall of the end platform shelter has been built to the level of the shelter's

lower surface. The tall shelter over platforms 4–11 runs 165 metres, serving most of the passengers of the long-distance trains and some of the commuting trains. A considerable number of the commuter passengers will be serviced by some 65 metres of lower shelters over platforms 1–4.

The steel structures of the tall platform shelter as well as the steel tension rods have been constructed of painted steel. The design has used annealed glass on the side of most platforms and over the tracks. The wiring for the lighting and public address systems has been installed in the solid parts of the shelter. The columns of the tall

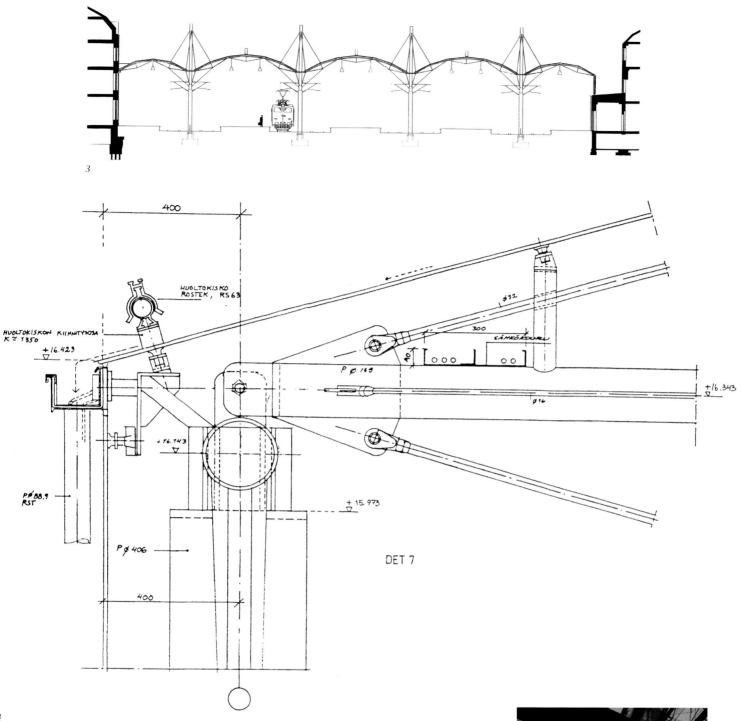

3

HUOLTOKISKO
ROSTEK, RS63

HUOLTOKISKON KIIHNITYSOSA
K ≈ 1350

+16.423

Pø 159

+16.343

Pø 88.9
RST

+16.143

+15.973

ø16

ø32

300

SÄHKÖKOURU

40

DET 7

Pø 406

400

4

platform shelter have been mounted on
foundations laid on existing steel pipe piles
between the tracks. The shelter has been supported
on the external walls of the station building on the
east and west sides.

The second stage of the project is due for
completion mid-2001.

5

CANOPY, CURTAINWALL AND WAVE

EMMIS COMMUNICATIONS WORLD HEADQUARTERS, INDIANAPOLIS, INDIANA, USA
RATIO Architects, Inc.

1

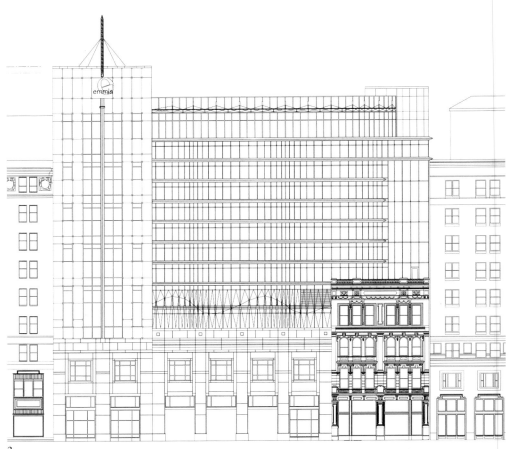

2

1 Building view from northeast
2 Building elevation
3 Seventh floor ornamental canopy plan and
   elevation
4 Seventh floor ornamental canopy section
5 Seventh floor ornamental canopy

The new seven-storey 13,192-square-metre corporate headquarters for Emmis Communications is located in the centre of Indianapolis, USA, on the southwest quadrant of Monument Circle. The design was inspired by the corporate logo, which is a skewed 'e' projecting beyond a square representing the corporate motto to 'think outside the box', and the AM and FM radiowave pattern representing communications.

Perhaps the most significant of the façades is the modern glass curtainwall. The seven-storey façade set back from the Monument Circle building edge, has created a forecourt while respecting the historic Journal façade. Themes of the radiowave

and communications are abstractly expressed in the curtainwall. Spacing of the vertical mullions varies, representing an FM radiowave pattern. A custom-metal trellis recalls the varying height of an AM radiowave pattern. The seventh floor is stepped back, creating an executive terrace featuring a translucent laminated glass canopy which creates a high-tech building cornice.

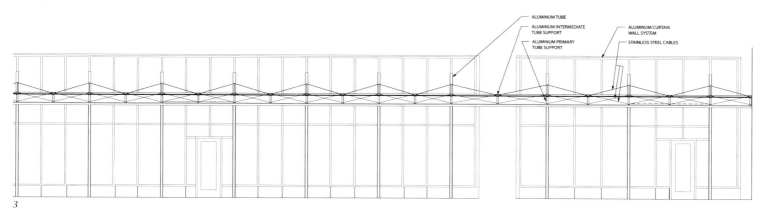

ALUMINUM TUBE
ALUMINUM INTERMEDIATE TUBE SUPPORT
ALUMINUM PRIMARY TUBE SUPPORT
ALUMINUM CURTAIN WALL SYSTEM
STAINLESS STEEL CABLES

3

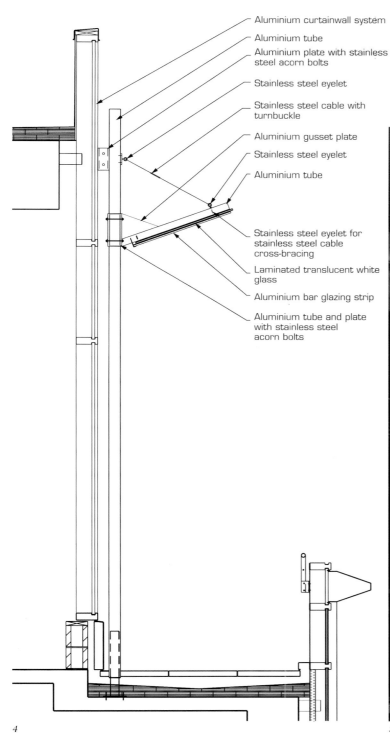

Aluminium curtainwall system

Aluminium tube

Aluminium plate with stainless steel acorn bolts

Stainless steel eyelet

Stainless steel cable with turnbuckle

Aluminium gusset plate

Stainless steel eyelet

Aluminium tube

Stainless steel eyelet for stainless steel cable cross-bracing

Laminated translucent white glass

Aluminium bar glazing strip

Aluminium tube and plate with stainless steel acorn bolts

4

5

6

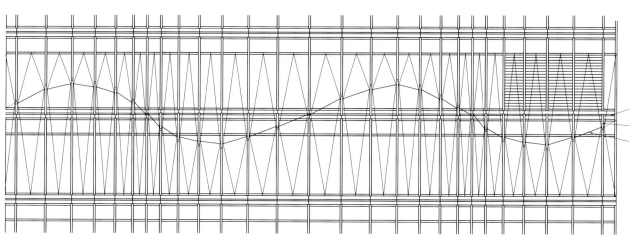

7

Aluminium curtair
system

Aluminium tube w
capped ends

Stainless steel ca
with turnbuckle,
centred

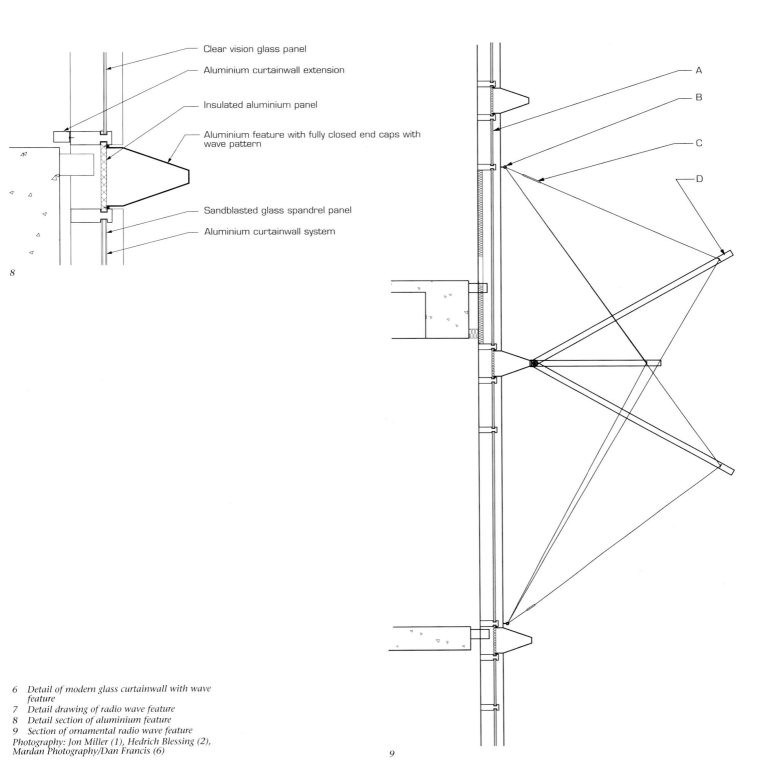

Clear vision glass panel

Aluminium curtainwall extension

Insulated aluminium panel

Aluminium feature with fully closed end caps with wave pattern

Sandblasted glass spandrel panel

Aluminium curtainwall system

8

6   Detail of modern glass curtainwall with wave
    feature
7   Detail drawing of radio wave feature
8   Detail section of aluminium feature
9   Section of ornamental radio wave feature
Photography: Jon Miller (1), Hedrich Blessing (2),
Mardan Photography/Dan Francis (6)

9

A

B

C

D

A   Aluminium curtainwall system
B   Stainless steel eyelet on horizontal
    mullion centred between vertical
    mullions
C   Stainless steel cable with turnbuckle,
    centred
D   Aluminium tube with capped ends

FACADE AND WALKWAY

WISHARD MEMORIAL HOSPITAL PARKING FACILITY, INDIANAPOLIS, INDIANA, USA
RATIO Architects, Inc.

1

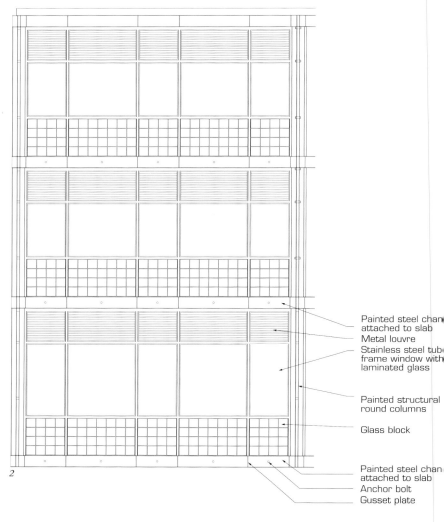

2

Painted steel chan
attached to slab
Metal louvre
Stainless steel tub
frame window with
laminated glass

Painted structural
round columns

Glass block

Painted steel chan
attached to slab
Anchor bolt
Gusset plate

This 1,200-car, six-level parking structure was the first building from a master plan designed to give the Wishard Memorial Hospital Complex a new image. The client initially requested that the parking structure have a brick façade that did not look like a car park. The structure relates to the scale and character of the adjacent historic hospital, apartment buildings, and contemporary university campus with its red brick, limestone detailing and four-storey height.

Designed to look like a laboratory building with punched window openings, it reveals itself as a car park at vertical openings near the corners, vehicle

entries, the expressed light poles on the roof and the painted metal railing details at the window openings.

The north elevation is the primary entrance and faces the main entry of the hospital. The enclosed cantilevered façade on the north has been created in response to several issues including the appropriate provision of parking space and walkways for people with disabilities.

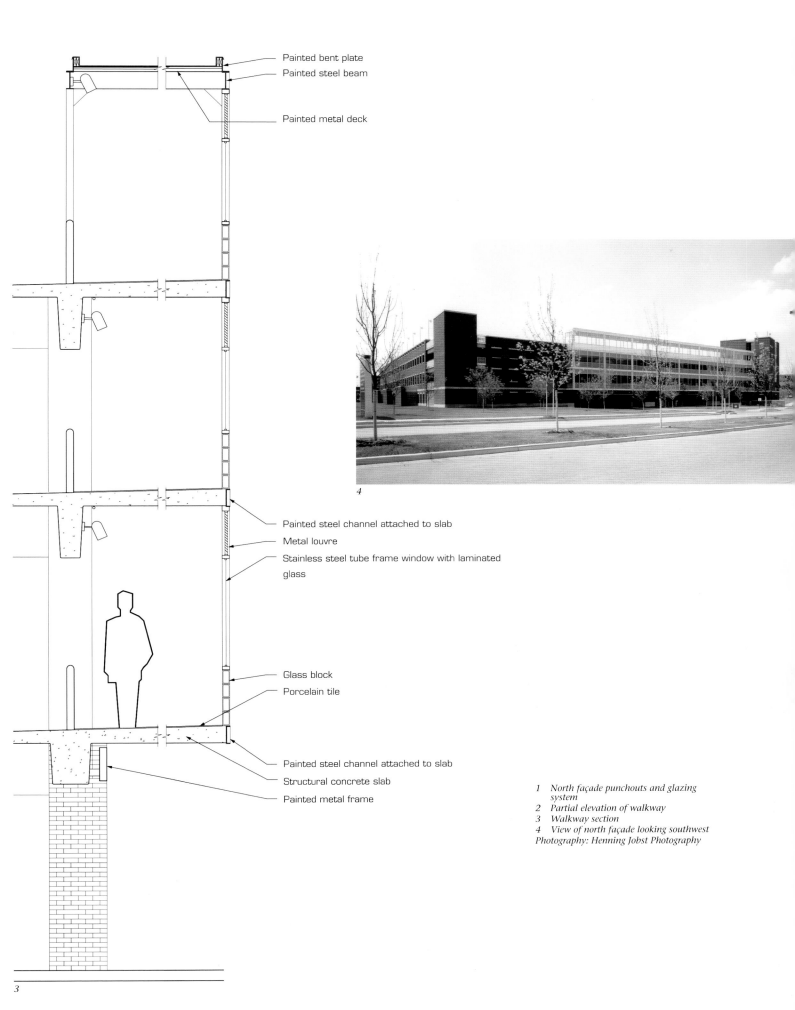

Painted bent plate
Painted steel beam

Painted metal deck

Painted steel channel attached to slab

Metal louvre

Stainless steel tube frame window with laminated
glass

Glass block
Porcelain tile

Painted steel channel attached to slab

Structural concrete slab

Painted metal frame

1   North façade punchouts and glazing
    system
2   Partial elevation of walkway
3   Walkway section
4   View of north façade looking southwest
Photography: Henning Jobst Photography

3

ROOF AND TRUSSES

VIRGINIA HOUSE, MONTROSE, VIRGINIA, USA
Rose Architecture

1

2

1 *View of studio across lake showing autumn*
   colours
2 *Side view of studio*
3 *Side elevation*
4 *Axonometric*

Commanding a lake view, this recreational retreat and art studio is an expression of the personality of a specific site and client. Very much like the historical villa typology, the meaning of the building is grounded in an idealised and narrative relationship of space, nature and time.

The densely wooded hill overlooks a lake and waterfowl sanctuary. Designed for a watercolour artist, the painting metaphors of colour, emersion and time characterise the essentially axial unfolding of landscape to water. In response to the aqueous essence of the painting process and the presence of the lake, the studio is a metaphorical vessel in which light is the contained element of value.

The main spaces of the entertainment and display area, entry gallery and painting studio are in a linear arrangement respectively from the top of the narrow site.

The passage from entry to the unobstructed view accentuates this order by approaching along the side of the building, traversing at the centre and then aligning with the axis. The site and building are revealed and unfold simultaneously, arriving at concentric steps that descend into the studio in the manner of waves lapping at the water's edge far below.

The strategy of constructing a vase of masonry, allowed a working platform from which to

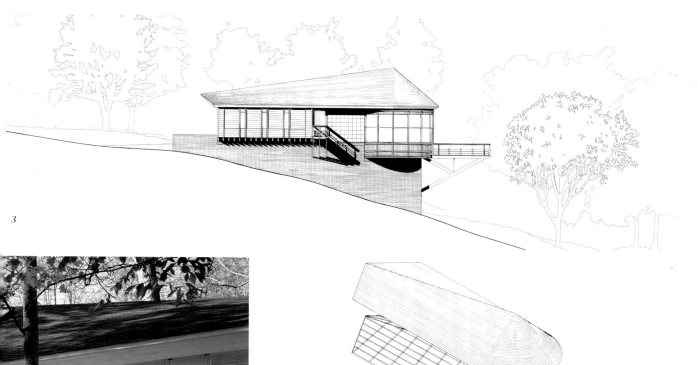

3

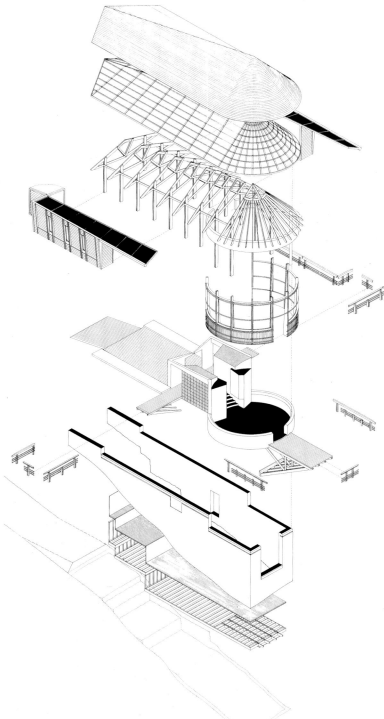

fabricate and express a series of enclosing spaces under a monolithic roof form and articulated structural truss system.

This composition system of objects on a pedestal modulates the slope of the terrain to allow a vehicular ramp into the building for the transport of art and the support of projecting balconies into the canopy of surrounding trees. The vocabulary of wood framing and cladding elements afforded a flexibility of form, in the parabolic roof and the curved walls of the cylindrical studio space, and is visually weighted by the volumetric mass of the brick and slateclad supporting walls.

4

5 *Elevation*
6 *Axonometric view through roof*
Opposite:
  Night view from balcony

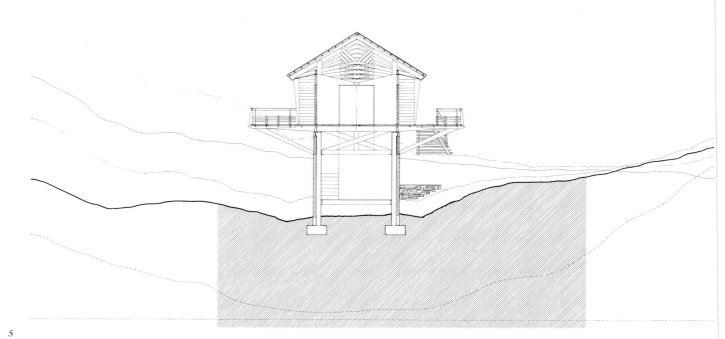

5

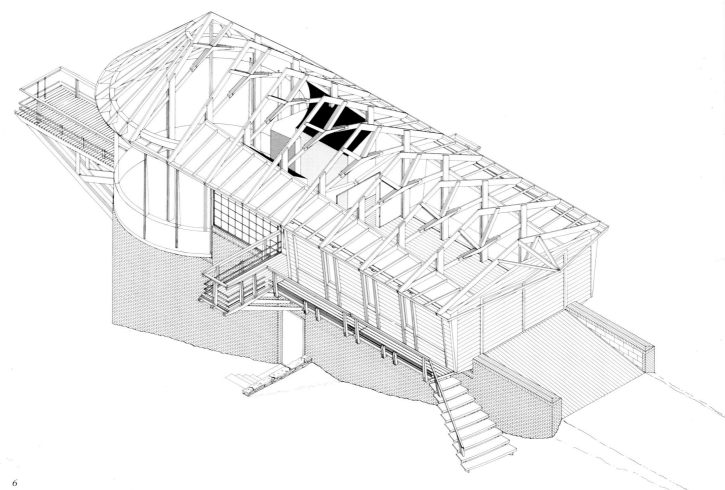

6

8   *View between side landings*
9   *View through house from balcony*
10&11   *Drawing showing roof trusses*
12   *Interior view showing trusses*
Photography: Prakash Patel

8

9

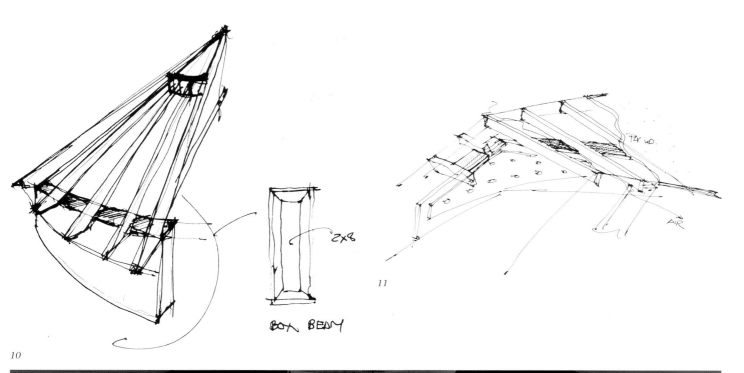

10

11

2×8

BOX BEAM

12

WALL SYSTEM

ATTIK, SAN FRANCISCO, CALIFORNIA, USA
Rose Architecture

1

1   Workspace area
2   Wall system elevation
3   Wall system

This interior landscape of transparent and opaque walls is situated in an existing 370-square-metre upper floor space in downtown San Francisco. Designed for an advertising agency, the interior architecture is sited within the industrial aesthetic of galvanised windows and exposed brick from the late 19th century.

The delineating and segmented wall was conceived as a ribbon of translucency that wraps and edges the various rooms as it flows through the existing office shell forming a bar/reception area, meeting and work areas with matching furniture.

Fabricated and installed by the architect, the wall elements have been made from anodised aluminium tube and angle sections that hold

in place a series of jalousie-type acrylic panels that alternate in colour and translucency.

Reflecting the client's desire for a work environment that would mirror and highlight a sense of lightness, this layering offers a projection of the human activity occurring in the space and a view through the entire volume. Within this system there are a number of openings where the panel system is hinged to operate as doors or moveable door panels.

The 4.6-metre-tall aluminium vertical support elements modulate the scale of the open space in addition to the rhythm of the connective elements that articulate the joinery of materials at a tactile scale.

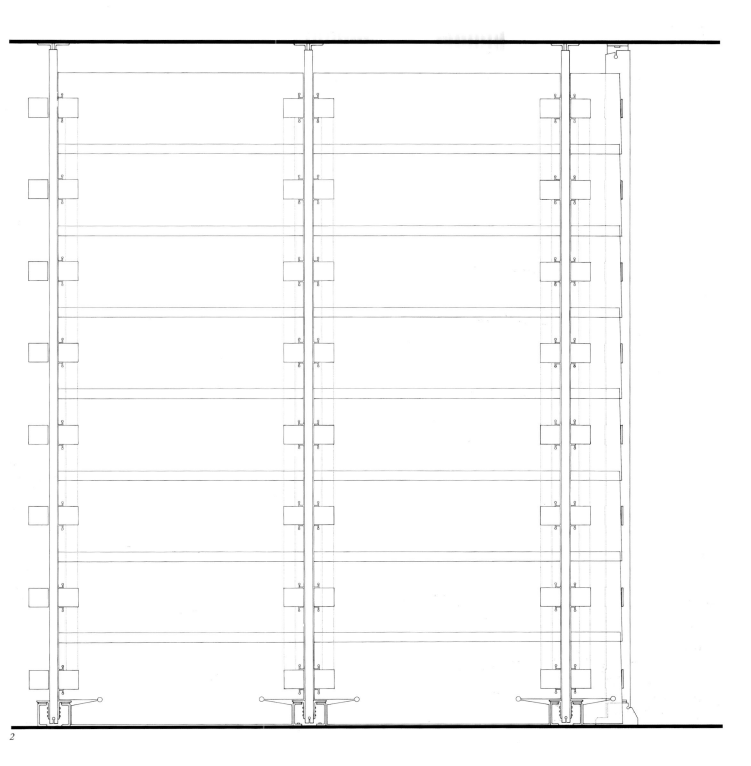

2

The entirety of assembled pieces were fabricated from stock aluminium that have been bolted together and reflects the process of their manufacture through the expression of cuts and drill holes.

The furnishings were designed to complement the wall system and were fabricated from welded steel, metal laminated plywood and metallic vinyl coverings for the bar stools.

The lightness of the material pallet allows the floor, walls and ceiling of the space to extend beyond the foreground towards a sense of ambiguity.

3

4&7 Workspace area
  5 Aluminium vertical support
  6 Detail elevation of wall system

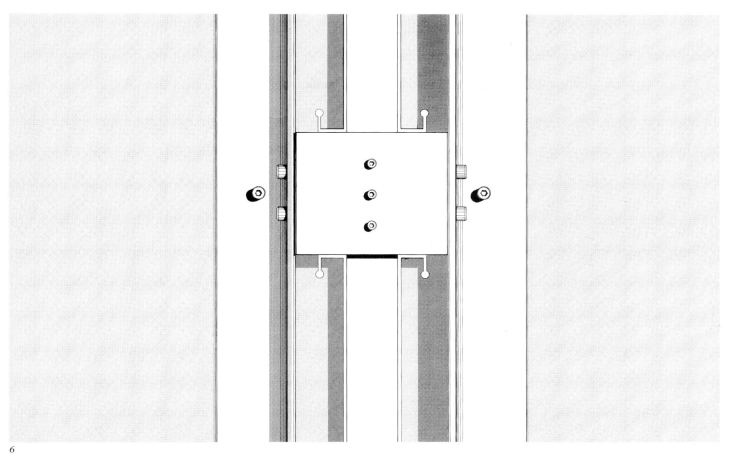

6

7

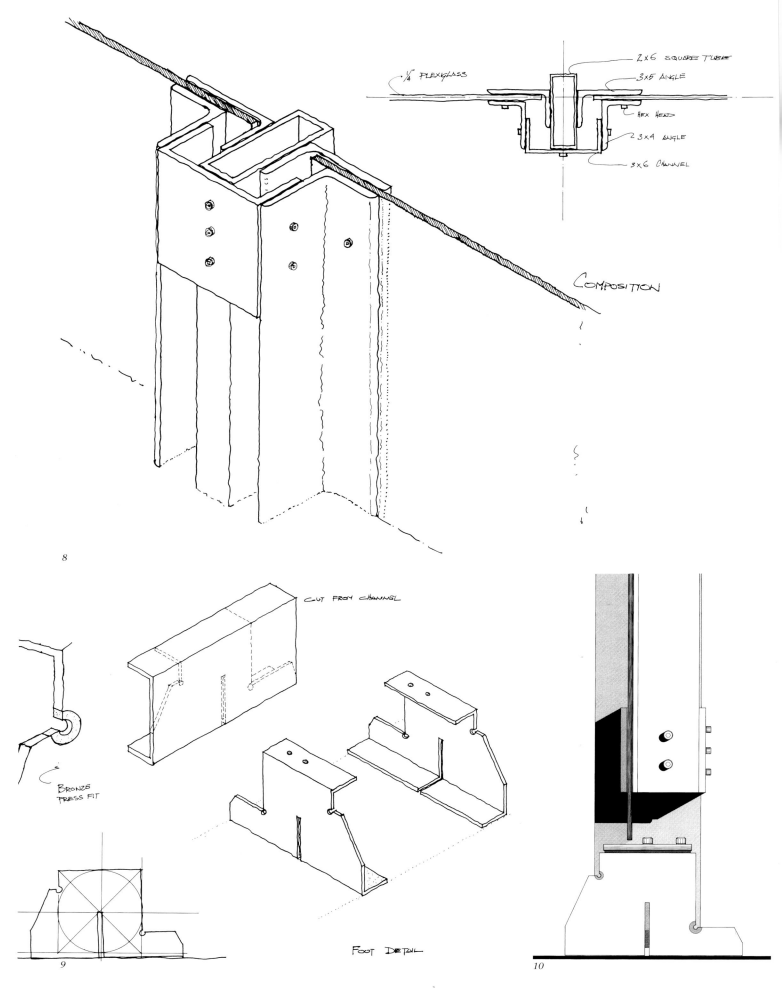

¼" PLEXGLASS

2×6 SQUARE TUBE

3×5 ANGLE

HEX HEAD

2 3×4 ANGLE

3×6 CHANNEL

COMPOSITION

8

CUT FROM CHANNEL

BRONZE
PRESS FIT

9

FOOT DETAIL

10

182

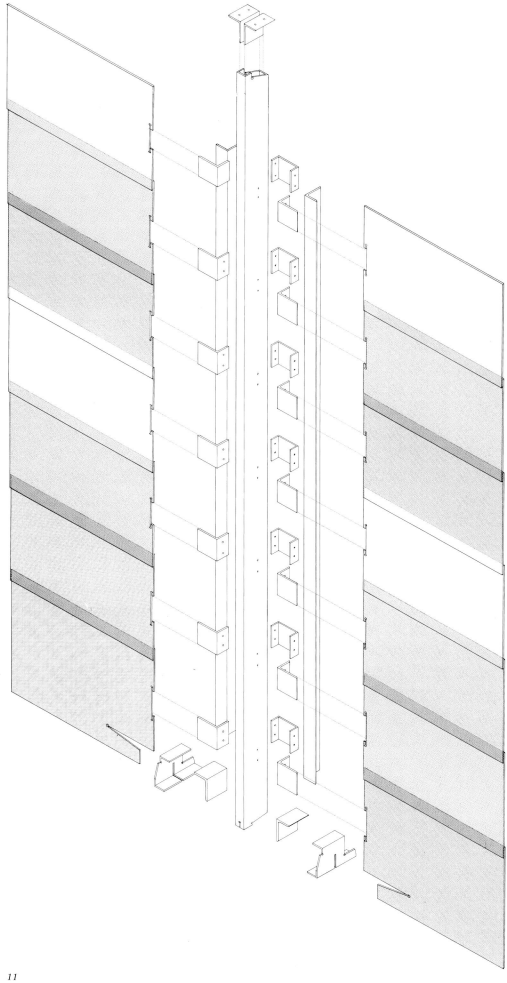

11

12

13

LOUVRES

EUROPEAN HEADQUARTERS OF LEVI STRAUSS, BRUSSELS, BELGIUM
Samyn and Partners

1

The project has been set within a development along the Brussels-Luxembourg railway line and near the campuses of two universities.

It is divided into two distinct volumes – one rectangular at the rear and the other following the curve in the road.

The junction of the two volumes features two vertical circulation cores that contain the elevators, stairs and mechanical shafts. The elevators face directly into the courtyard and are protected by a façade comprising glass louvres. The precast concrete landings and stairways take advantage of the natural light, which the louvres provide.

1 Skyward view of courtyard
2 Louvre detail
3&4 Internal courtyard featuring
    louvred façade
Photography: Serge Brison, (1,3); Ch Bastin and J Evrard, (4)

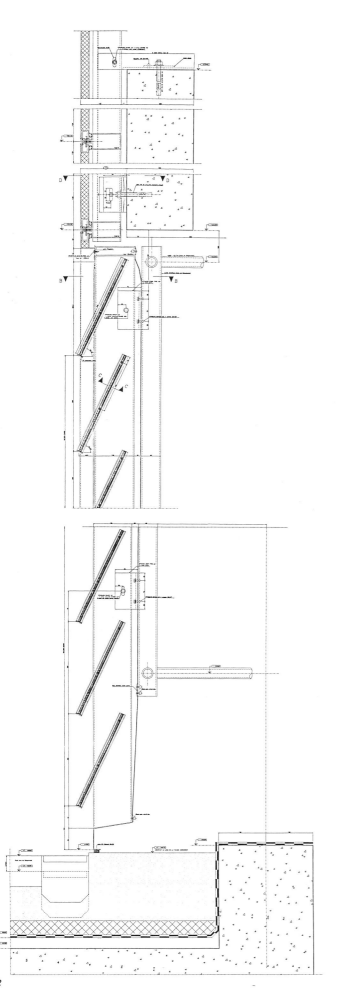

2

3

4

ARCED WALL

GROUND ZERO POST PRODUCTION, MARINA DEL REY, CALIFORNIA, USA
Shubin + Donaldson Architects

1

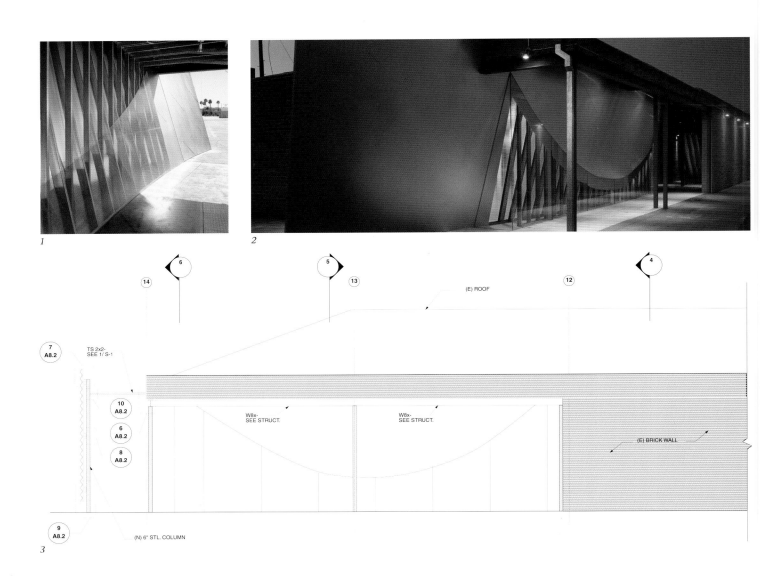

2

3

This post-production facility occupies a former light manufacturing warehouse adjacent to its ad agency headquarters. The client called for an open plan with six editing bays, reception area, kitchen and gathering spaces.

The main conference room is defined by an arcing wall that extends through to the exterior and forms the entry vestibule.

The two buildings are separated by an alley, but have been connected in design detail – for example, prefabricated trusses have been included in the new facility for conceptual consistency. A rhythmic repetition of tightly spaced metal trusses

forms the dramatic circulation spine that travels the entire length of the building.

The basic open-plan workspace is continually intersected by arcing aluminium-clad walls that weave in and throughout the floor plan. These bold architectural statements have resulted in a series of abstracted and dynamically shaped volumes that are used as meeting rooms, editing bays, display nooks, kitchen and passageways.

4

1   Detail view of arcing wall that extends
    through glass wall from main conference
    room to outside
2   Exterior view of entrance with arcing
    aluminium-clad walls that weave
    throughout workspace
3   Exterior elevation plan
4   Arcing aluminium wall extends from
    exterior through inside of facility, which
    separates main conference room to left,
    and entrance to right
5   Floor plan
Photography: Tom Bonner

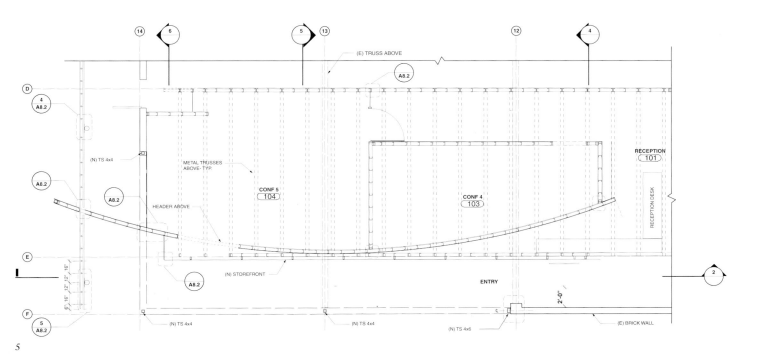

5

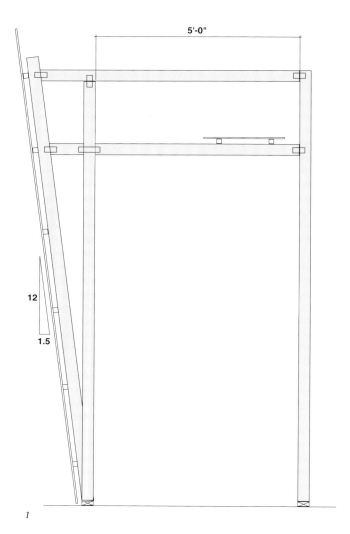

1

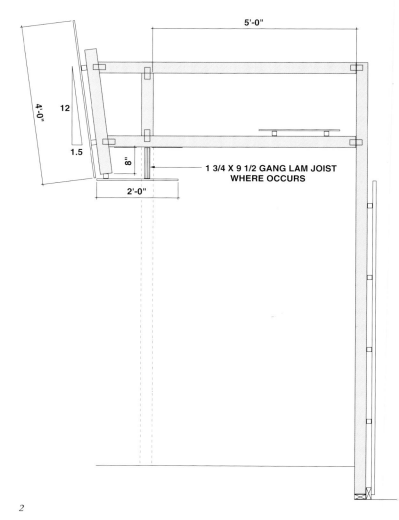

1 3/4 X 9 1/2 GANG LAM JOIST WHERE OCCURS

2

1,2,4&5   Sections through informational tract
3   Overview of work room illustrating raw material used
6   Detailed view of wiring and raw materials used outside work room hallway
7   Rendering of informational tract
Photography: Farshid Assassi

This 743-square-metre loft space has been redesigned for Fuel Design & Production, creating a fun but serious environment that reflects the working culture of the company.

The design has combined and contrasted the basic raw industrial look of the original warehouse. The studio features transparent conduits for carrying computer wiring and cables that emphasise how the latest technology functions at Fuel. Translucent panels also feature in the space, not only allowing light to pass through, but also acting as screens upon which Fuel can project changing images of its work. Much of the main shell of the existing warehouse was left intact and exposed.

The architects generated a 'design attitude' from the planning stages, reflecting the creative culture of Fuel: raw, spontaneous, flexible and intentional. The program, bolstered by extensive notes from the client, has called for maximum design creativity and impact at minimum cost. Other features of the design include editing bays, animation and production zones, two conference rooms, both small offices and executive private offices, and a wide-open activity area with indoor basketball hoop, kitchen and lounge area.

3

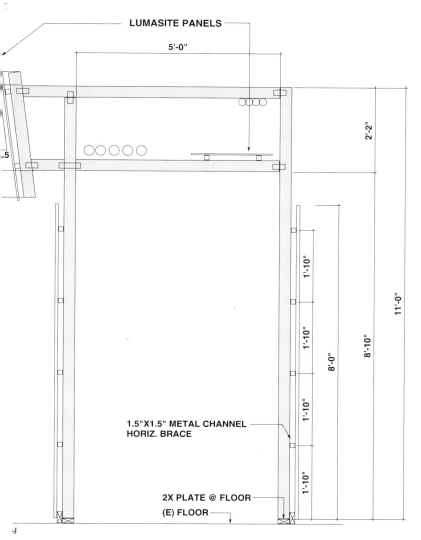

LUMASITE PANELS

5'-0"

2'-2"

1'-10"

1'-10"

8'-0"

8'-10"

11'-0"

1'-10"

1.5"X1.5" METAL CHANNEL
HORIZ. BRACE

1'-10"

2X PLATE @ FLOOR

(E) FLOOR

4

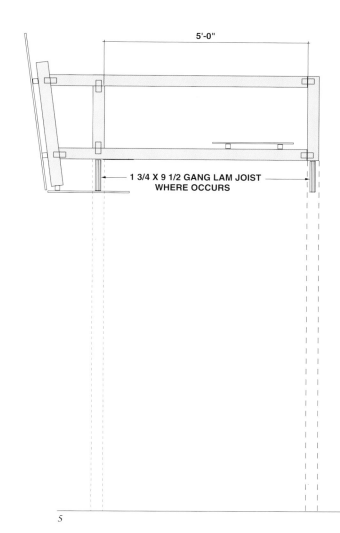

5'-0"

1 3/4 X 9 1/2 GANG LAM JOIST
WHERE OCCURS

5

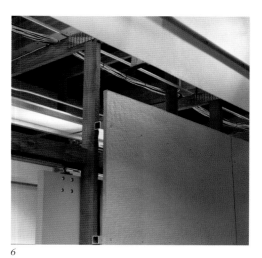

6

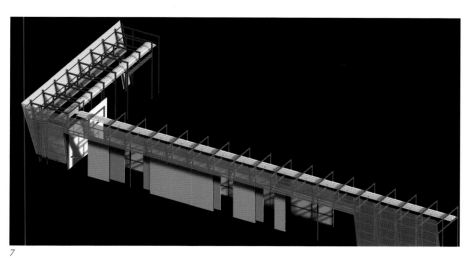

7

PANEL WALLS

IWIN.COM, WESTWOOD, CALIFORNIA, USA
Shubin + Donaldson Architects

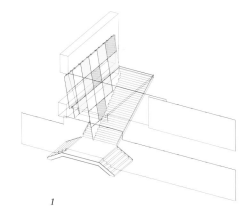

1

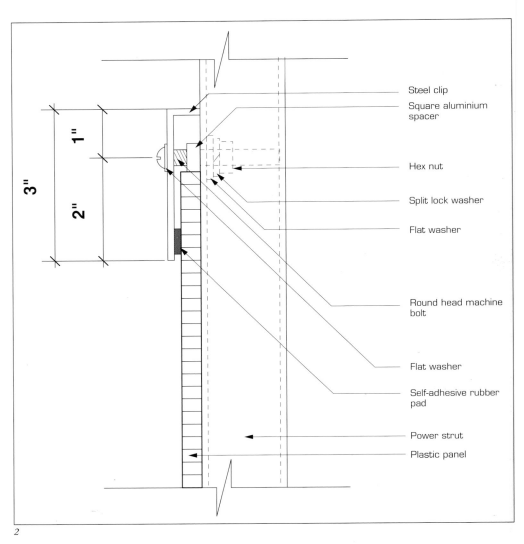

Steel clip

Square aluminium spacer

Hex nut

Split lock washer

Flat washer

Round head machine bolt

Flat washer

Self-adhesive rubber pad

Power strut

Plastic panel

2

The client wanted a new office space to reflect its active and successful website. The architectural design team was asked to build a flexible workspace that expands and contracts periodically, depending on workload, to accommodate a young staff of engineers, programmers, marketeers and executives. The offices needed to reflect its online presence.

The plan included a loft-like, industrial and open space despite the office tower setting. To create this atmosphere within a challenging floor plan, the enclosed spaces, such as conference rooms, storage, kitchen and massage room, have been attached

entirely to the already existing solid walled core in the middle of the space. This has allowed for open space around the perimeter, while maximising natural light.

Brightly coloured Plexiglas panels accent the industrial building materials chosen to give the space a sense of modernism. An interior stairway, with walls of yellow, orange, white and clear acrylic sheeting, functions as an informal gathering space as well as for circulation.

The workstations have been custom designed from aluminium sheeting with bright-green rolling file standards. A power strut grid in the ceiling with

3

hanging flexible power channels allows the stations to be reconfigured according to need. Conference room and corridor walls are faced with white markerboard.

The client's visual website presence has been mirrored with the use of its corporate colour, intense lime green, and playing it against other colours, transparency and opacity.

1   Entry stairway axons of Plexiglas-panel
    wall from two different views
2   Clip detail of Plexiglas-panel installation
3   View of interior stairway with yellow,
    orange, white and clear Plexiglas-panel
    walls
Photography: Tom Bonner

RAMP AND SCRIM

GROUND ZERO, MARINA DEL REY, CALIFORNIA, USA
Shubin + Donaldson Architects

1

The interior design of this 930-square-metre loft space features a spectacular processionary 2.9-metre-high ramp leading from the elevated second-floor glass-enclosed entry.

As guests, clients and staff make their way down the ramp and through the working 'hall' they are treated to an ever changing palette of the agency's work projected on a series of theatrical scrims spanning the width of the space.

The interior was left raw and exposed with sandblasted concrete walls and a bow-truss ceiling. Existing concrete floors have been sealed and interior 'war rooms' at the perimeter have been

added with architectural elements to express a sense of 'interior village'.

The architects have designed steel workstations with industrial light fixtures, file storage and desktop organisers that park side-by-side across the space. A loft level houses the library, video/editing bays and focus-group rooms.

The 6.1-metre-high exterior ramp brings entrants into the building from a private parking lot via a glass-encased vestibule that leads to the corresponding interior ramp.

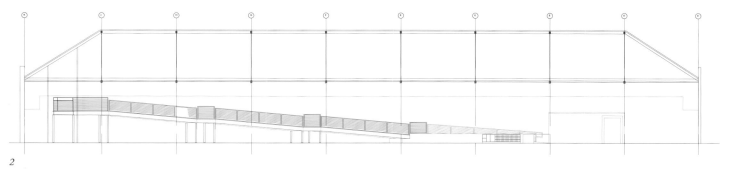

2

3

4

The space is extremely engaging, thanks to the large-scale unbroken loft-like environment. The custom-designed workstations recall the industrial set design of Orson Welles' movies and the early Fritz Lang masterpiece, *Metropolis*.

Important elements have been included in the design to encourage creativity and workflow. The design includes strategic areas for working, with mini-think tanks for focus groups, and privacy for concentration and creation.

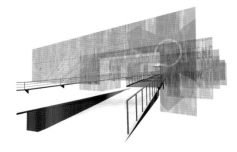

5

1   View of ramp leading through office
2   Building section of exterior ramp entrance
3   Exterior ramp guiding entrants into building through glass-encased vestibule
4   Overview of workstations, ramp, and interior shell of building
5   Digital rendering of theatrical scrim
Photography: Tom Bonner

ROOF
HONG KONG CONVENTION & EXHIBITION CENTER
Skidmore, Owings & Merrill LLP (SOM)

1

2

The dramatic 150,000-square-metre extension of the Hong Kong Convention & Exhibition Centre was built as an addition to the original facility. The extension is intended as a symbol for Hong Kong: the roof shape expresses flight, and represents the dramatic evolution of Hong Kong and its new role as the gateway to China.

Curvilinear building forms have been created by a wing-like roof. Metal and glass banding in the curtain walls reinforce the curved geometry and horizontal expression, and provide a contrast to the cubic and vertical nature of Hong Kong's rectilinear skyline.

As the predominant feature of the extension, the roof measures over 40,000 square metres and serves as the ceiling for the entire extension. The roof form is expressed as a series of intersecting curved wings that are shaped by the requirements of the structure and by the clear span over the convention and upper exhibition halls.

The façade is layered to echo the functional zones within and is modulated along its length to contrast screenlike zones with areas of transparency at the lobby and convention hall pre-function areas. The latter are supported by cable trusses and allow panoramic views of Victoria Harbour.

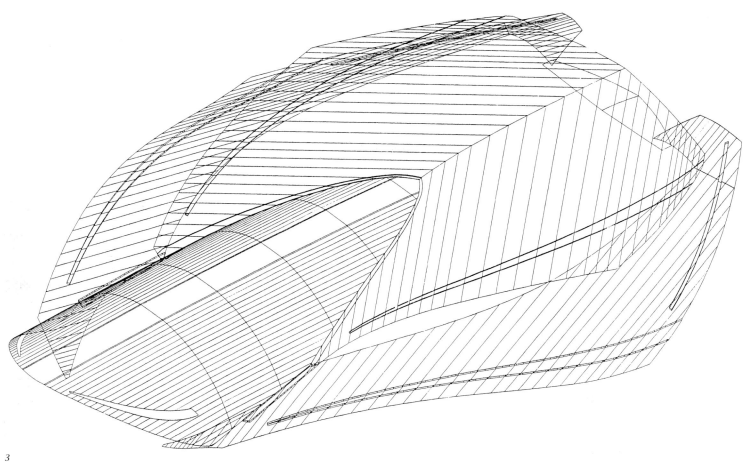

3

The extension includes a 4,500-seat convention hall, three exhibition halls, pre-function areas, support facilities and restaurants. An atrium link spans over the water channel and future expressway, connecting the new convention centre to the existing exhibition spaces at four levels. The link also provides additional overflow exhibition space.

4

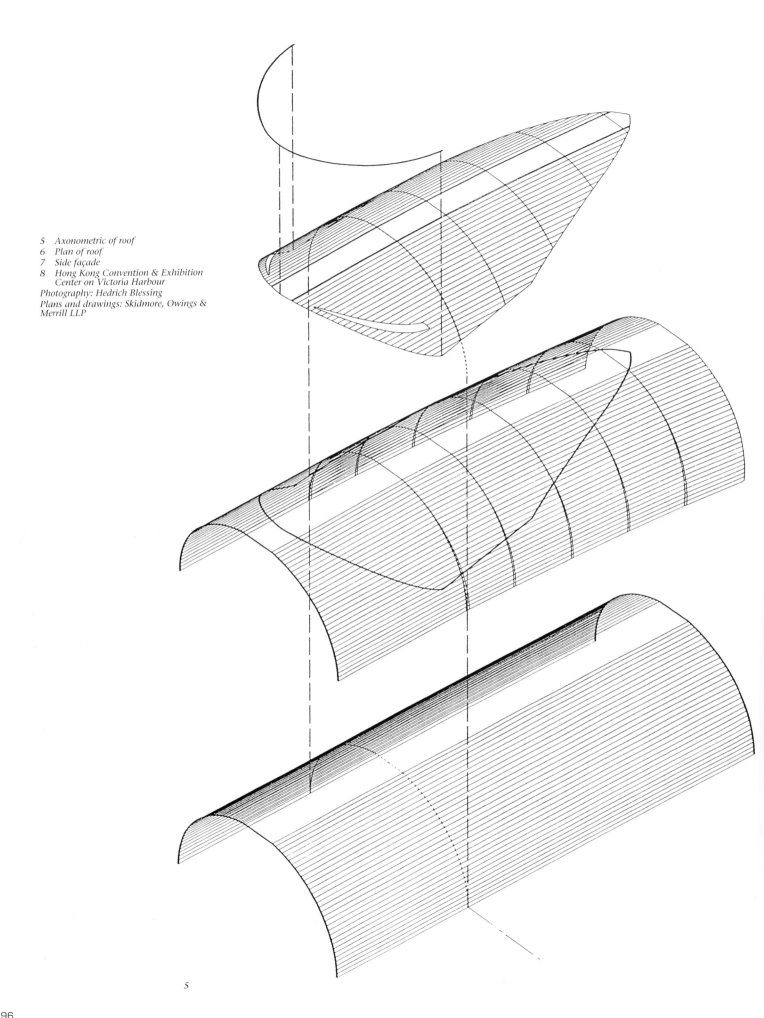

5   *Axonometric of roof*
6   *Plan of roof*
7   *Side façade*
8   *Hong Kong Convention & Exhibition*
    Center on Victoria Harbour
Photography: Hedrich Blessing
Plans and drawings: Skidmore, Owings &
Merrill LLP

5

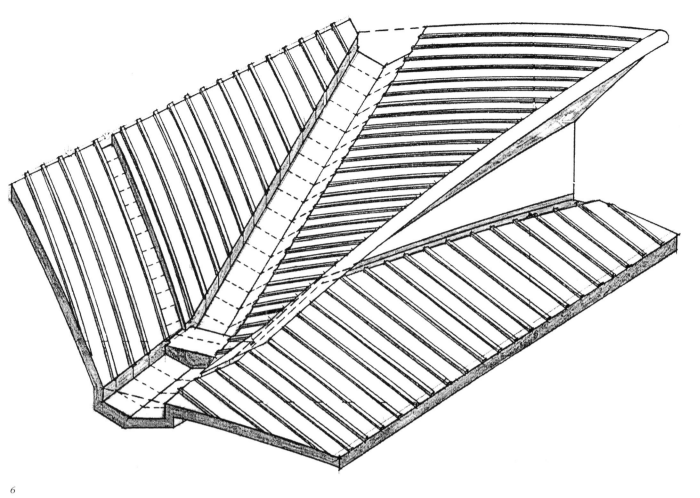

6

7

8

SKYLIGHT

MAYAN NETWORKS, SAN JOSE, CALIFORNIA, USA
STUDIOS Architecture

1

3 5/8 inch track, typ

Translucent acrylic
panels (above)

3/8 inch aluminium
edge channel

7/8 inch horizontal hat
channels above, typ

Sheet metal fasteners
with exposed grommets,
typ (above)

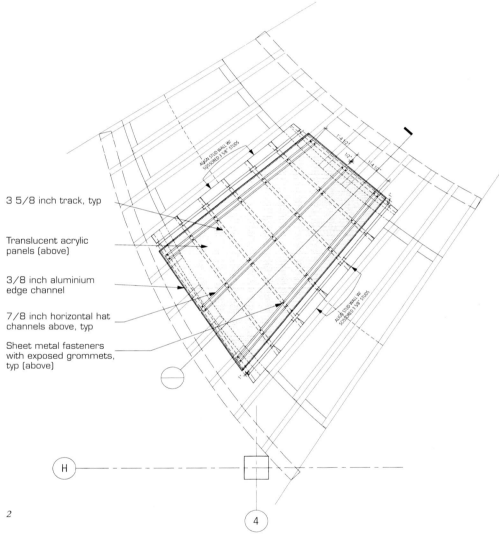

H

2

4

1 Entrance to central gathering space
2 Detail of plan view
3 Floorplan of ovoid kiva
4 Skylights illuminate crux of crisscrossing
   metal studs

In a world dominated by partitions and cubicles, the headquarters of Mayan Networks has been designed to improve communication and encourage a sense of community amongst employees.

The centrally located ovoid was inspired by a native American *kiva* – a central gathering space for community members to meet and interact. The gathering space measures 131 square metres.

Four 1.82-square-metre skylights were added above the crux of the crisscrossing 9.2-centimetre unpunched metal studs, which naturally illuminate a once dark area at the core of the building. The studs are sheathed with translucent corrugated fibreglass that reveals the skeleton within and creates a dynamic play of light that continually glows and changes throughout the course of the day.

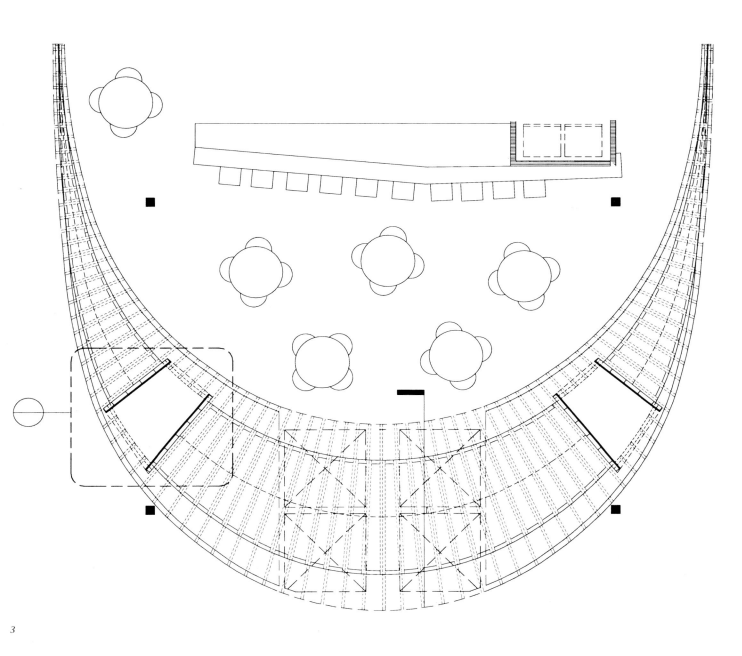

3

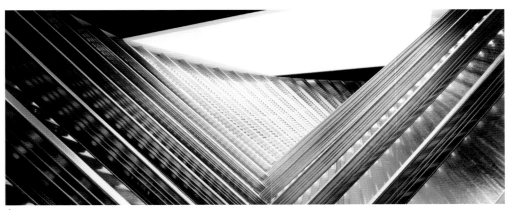

4

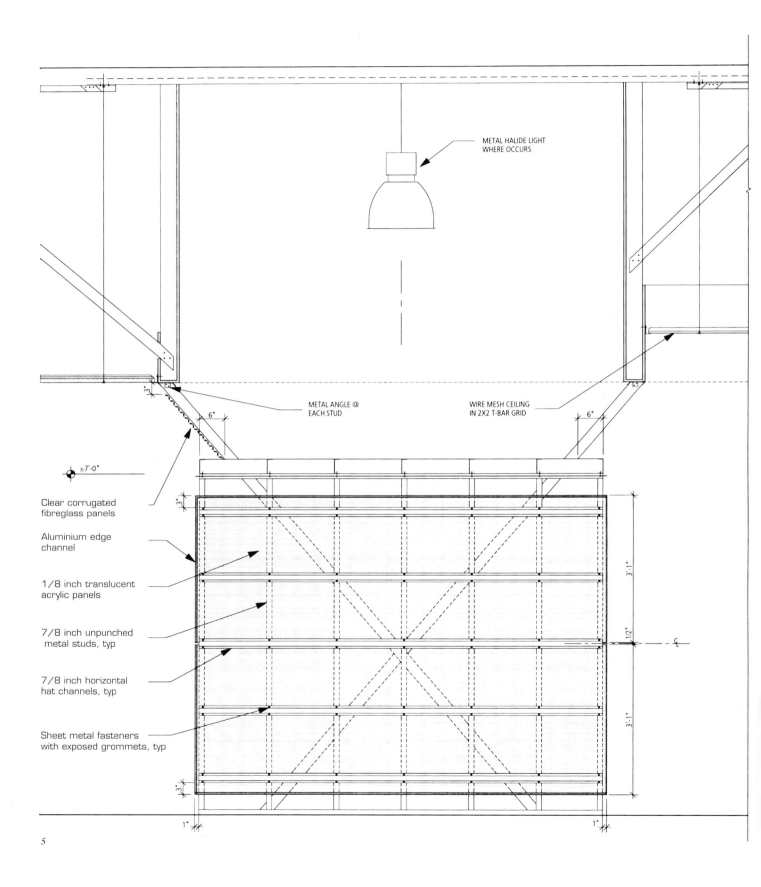

METAL HALIDE LIGHT
WHERE OCCURS

METAL ANGLE @
EACH STUD

WIRE MESH CEILING
IN 2X2 T-BAR GRID

±7'-0"

Clear corrugated
fibreglass panels

Aluminium edge
channel

1/8 inch translucent
acrylic panels

7/8 inch unpunched
metal studs, typ

7/8 inch horizontal
hat channels, typ

Sheet metal fasteners
with exposed grommets, typ

6"

6"

3"

3"

3'-1"

1/2"

3'-1"

3"

1"

1"

5

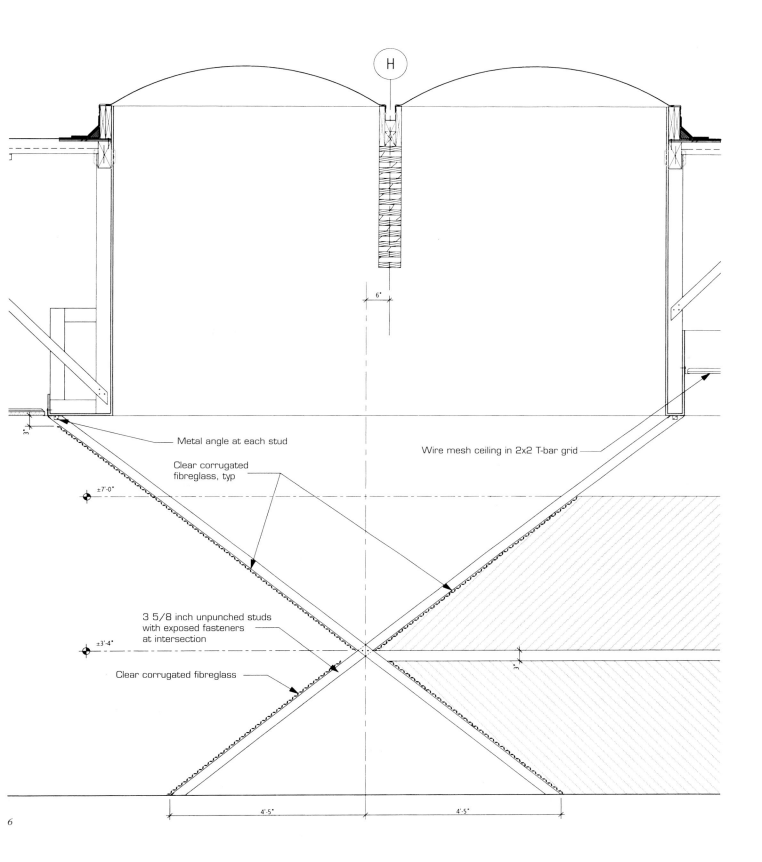

H

6"

Metal angle at each stud

Wire mesh ceiling in 2x2 T-bar grid

Clear corrugated
fibreglass, typ

±7'-0"

3"

3 5/8 inch unpunched studs
with exposed fasteners
at intersection

±3'-4"

3"

Clear corrugated fibreglass

4'-5"

4'-5"

6

GLAZED WALL

SMESTADDAMMEN PARK, OSLO WEST, NORWAY
Niels Torp AS Architects MNAL

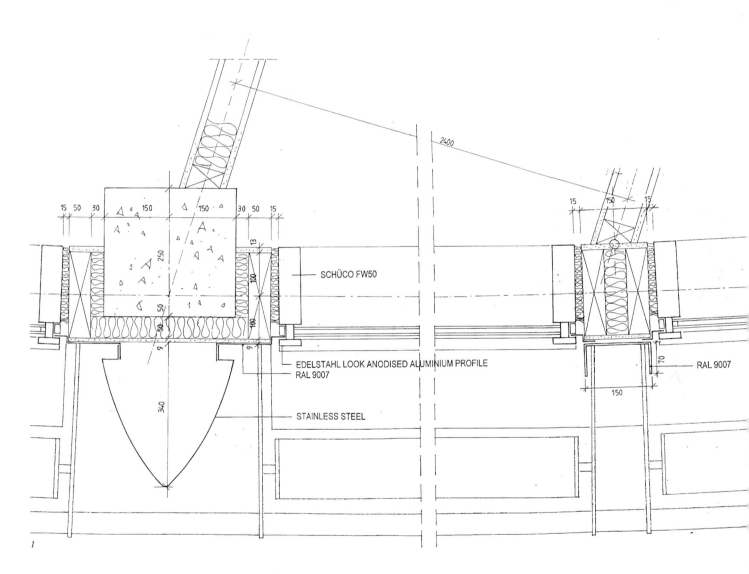

SCHÜCO FW50

EDELSTAHL LOOK ANODISED ALUMINIUM PROFILE
RAL 9007

STAINLESS STEEL

RAL 9007

1

2

Smestaddammen Park comprises three office buildings located next to a major ring road in Oslo West. Each building has two office wings gathered around a glass-covered atrium, with outward views provided through a vast glazed façade.

Building A opens towards the lake and parkland, and an exposed concrete grid in front of the glazing provides a stimulating play of light and shadow.

Building B has a curved façade of glass and metal, which forms the 'hub' of the development and conveys the development's directional changes.

Building C is oriented towards the panoramic views in the south. Window elements throughout the development consist of aluminium frames, anodised to resemble stainless steel, with spandrels of corrugated stainless steel behind silk-screened glass.

Glass dominates the atrium façade in building A and C to contrast with the brickwork exterior. Similarly, the glass and metal exterior in building B is replaced by a more solid brickwork appearance in the atrium.

3

4

1&5   *Glazed wall detail Building B*
2   *External glazed wall Building B*
3   *View across lake with Building A*
4   *Detail of glazed wall Building B*
Photography: courtesy of Niels Torp AS
Architects MNAL

The glazed atrium acts as the communication and social nucleus in each building; being flanked by libraries, staff canteens and conference facilities – with the lift/staircase towers forming airy vertical sculptures. The three atria have been designed with distinct differences in architectural expression and detailing.

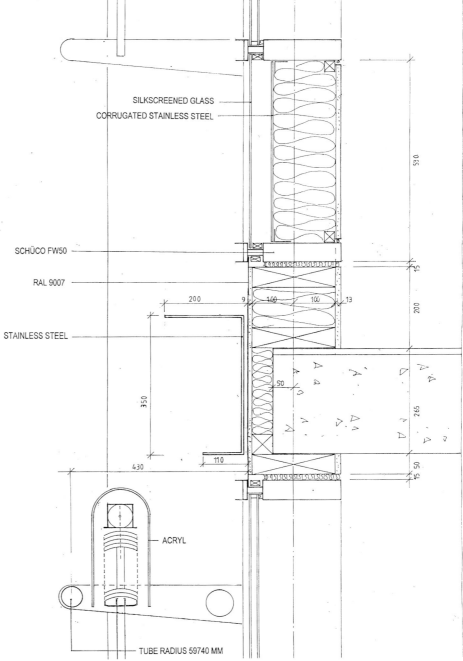

SILKSCREENED GLASS
CORRUGATED STAINLESS STEEL

SCHÜCO FW50

RAL 9007

STAINLESS STEEL

ACRYL

TUBE RADIUS 59740 MM

5

ANTENNA, AIRLOCK, CANOPY AND SUNSHADES

ELECTRONICS AND COMMUNICATION ENGINEERING, SINGAPORE POLYTECHNIC, REPUBLIC OF SINGAPORE

TSP Architects + Planners Pte Ltd

1

2

The building comprises three distinct volumes, with each volume responding to the adjoining context and use.

The first volume has been crowned with a rolling roof that slips off its ends to intensify the unstable state of the form; this added motion indicates a pedestrian movement in correspondence to the mass. The creeping roof has created two *termini* where one announces a ground approach from a public corridor and the other identifies a departure via a steel footbridge connected to a vertical transport core in bright chromatic colour.

Adjacent to the transport core rises a quadrant, the volume of which is transformed into a taller mass as it confronts a busy motorway.

The third volume consumes this transformation and completes the triangulated formation on a figure ground plan. In close proximity to a mutated retaining wall sustaining a photo-sensitive laboratory at the semi-basement, a grand staircase ascends to a sheltered court within. A series of apertures connects the court to the spaces beyond and unveils a different interactive experience that partially reveals the existing fabric of its neighbour.

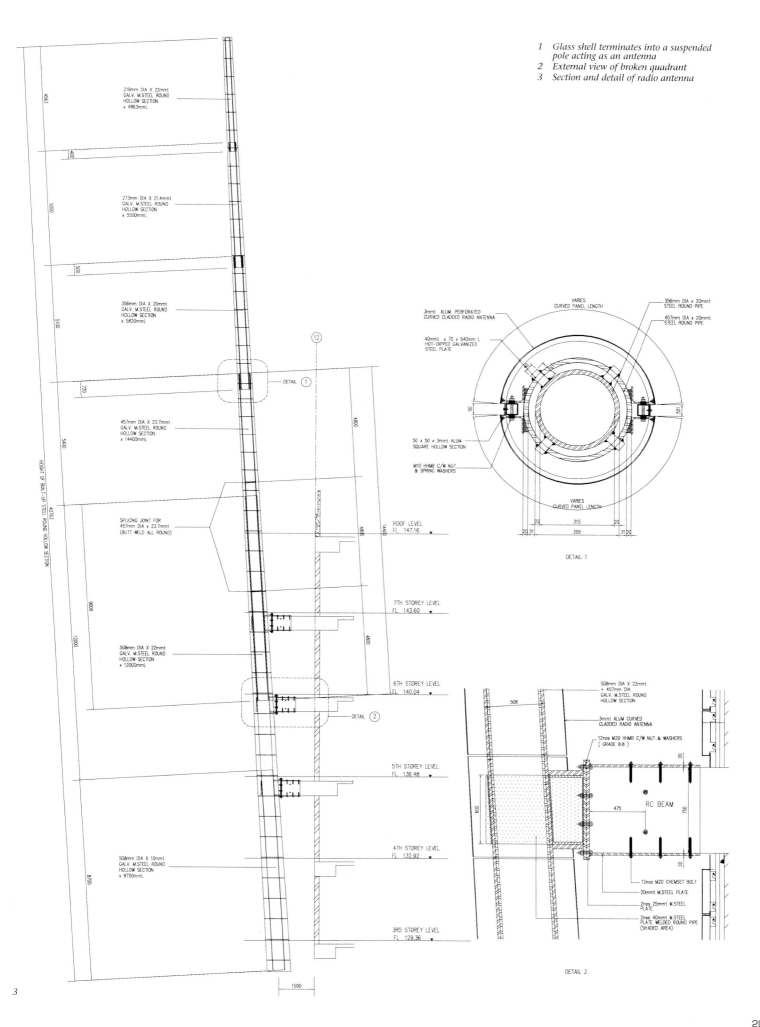

1 Glass shell terminates into a suspended
  pole acting as an antenna
2 External view of broken quadrant
3 Section and detail of radio antenna

219mm DIA X 22mmt
GALV. M.STEEL ROUND
HOLLOW SECTION
x 4963mmL

273mm DIA X 21.4mmt
GALV. M.STEEL ROUND
HOLLOW SECTION
x 5500mmL

356mm DIA X 20mmt
GALV. M.STEEL ROUND
HOLLOW SECTION
x 5820mmL

DETAIL 1

457mm DIA X 23.7mmt
GALV. M.STEEL ROUND
HOLLOW SECTION
x 14400mmL

SPLICING JOINT FOR
457mm DIA X 23.7mmt
(BUTT WELD ALL ROUND)

508mm DIA X 22mmt
GALV. M.STEEL ROUND
HOLLOW SECTION
x 12000mmL

DETAIL 2

508mm DIA X 10mmt
GALV. M.STEEL ROUND
HOLLOW SECTION
x 8700mmL

HEIGHT OF BUILT-UP STEEL ROUND HOLLOW SECTION

ROOF LEVEL
FL 147.16

7TH STOREY LEVEL
FL 143.60

6TH STOREY LEVEL
FL 140.04

5TH STOREY LEVEL
FL 136.48

4TH STOREY LEVEL
FL 132.92

3RD STOREY LEVEL
FL 129.36

3mmt ALUM. PERFORATED
CURVED CLADDED RADIO ANTENNA

40mmt x 70 x 640mm L
HOT-DIPPED GALVANIZED
STEEL PLATE

50 x 50 x 3mmt ALUM
SQUARE HOLLOW SECTION

M10 HHMB C/W NUT
& SPRING WASHERS

VARIES
CURVED PANEL LENGTH

356mm DIA x 20mmt
STEEL ROUND PIPE

457mm DIA X 20mmt
STEEL ROUND PIPE

VARIES
CURVED PANEL LENGTH

DETAIL 1

508mm DIA X 22mmt
+ 457mm DIA
GALV. M.STEEL ROUND
HOLLOW SECTION

3mmt ALUM CURVED
CLADDED RADIO ANTENNA

12nos M20 HHMB C/W NUT & WASHERS
(GRADE 8.8)

RC BEAM

12nos M20 CHEMSET BOLT

20mmt M.STEEL PLATE

2nos 25mmt M.STEEL
PLATE

2nos 40mmt M.STEEL
PLATE WELDED ROUND PIPE
(SHADED AREA)

DETAIL 2

3

4

5

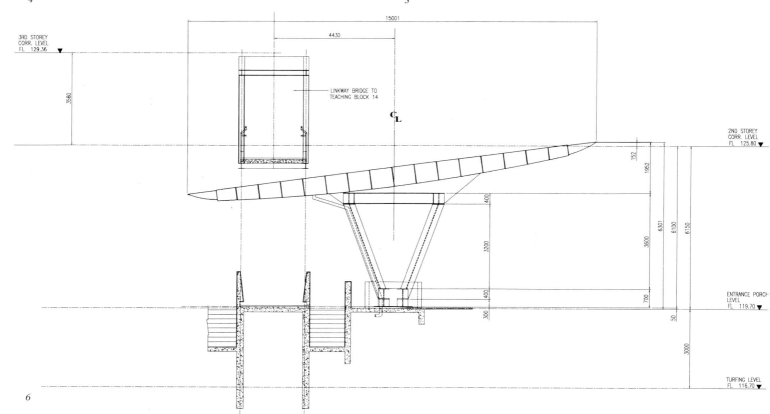

6

3RD STOREY
CORR. LEVEL
FL 129.36 ▼

3560

15001
4430

LINKWAY BRIDGE TO
TEACHING BLOCK 14

C**L**

2ND STOREY
CORR. LEVEL
FL 125.80 ▼

152
1952

400

6301
3200

6100

6150

3600

ENTRANCE PORCH
LEVEL
FL 119.70 ▼

400
300
700
50

3000

TURFING LEVEL
FL 116.70 ▼

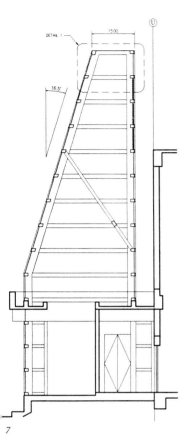

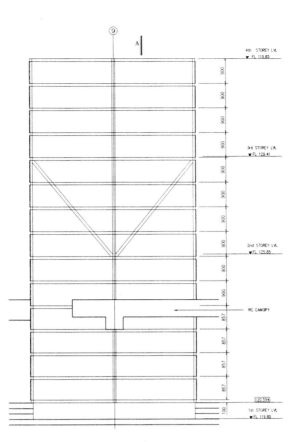

4&5 Canopy
6 Elevation of aluminium canopy
7 Detail of airlock
8 Interior view of airlock
9 External view of airlock

7

8

9

10

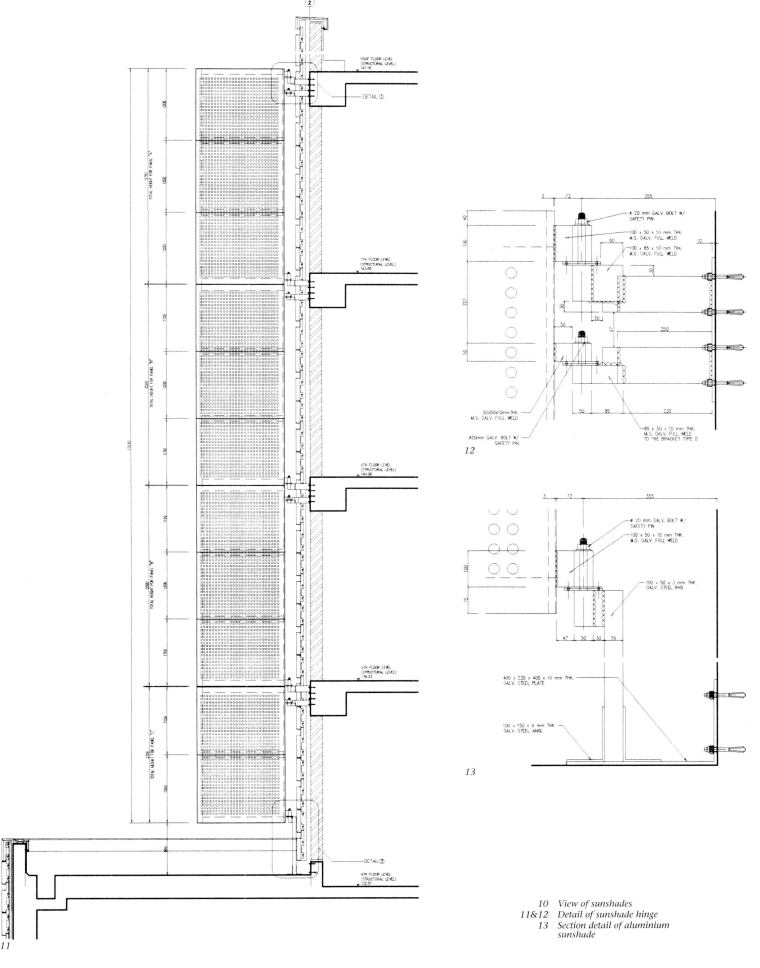

12

13

10 View of sunshades
11&12 Detail of sunshade hinge
13 Section detail of aluminium
    sunshade

11

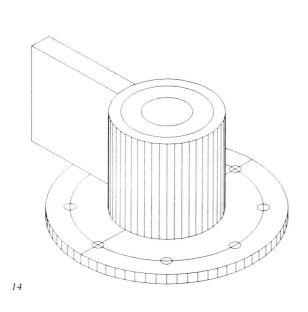

14

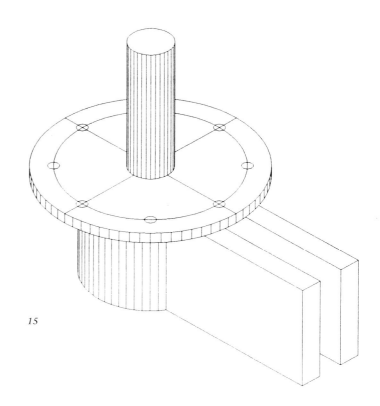

15

16

17

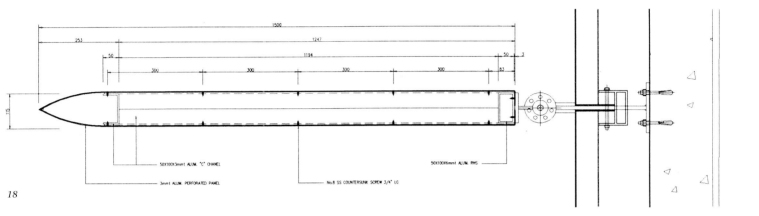

18

50X100X3mmt ALUM. "C" CHANEL

3mmt ALUM. PERFORATED PANEL

50X100X6mmt ALUM. RHS

No.8 SS COUNTERSUNK SCREW 3/4" LG

19

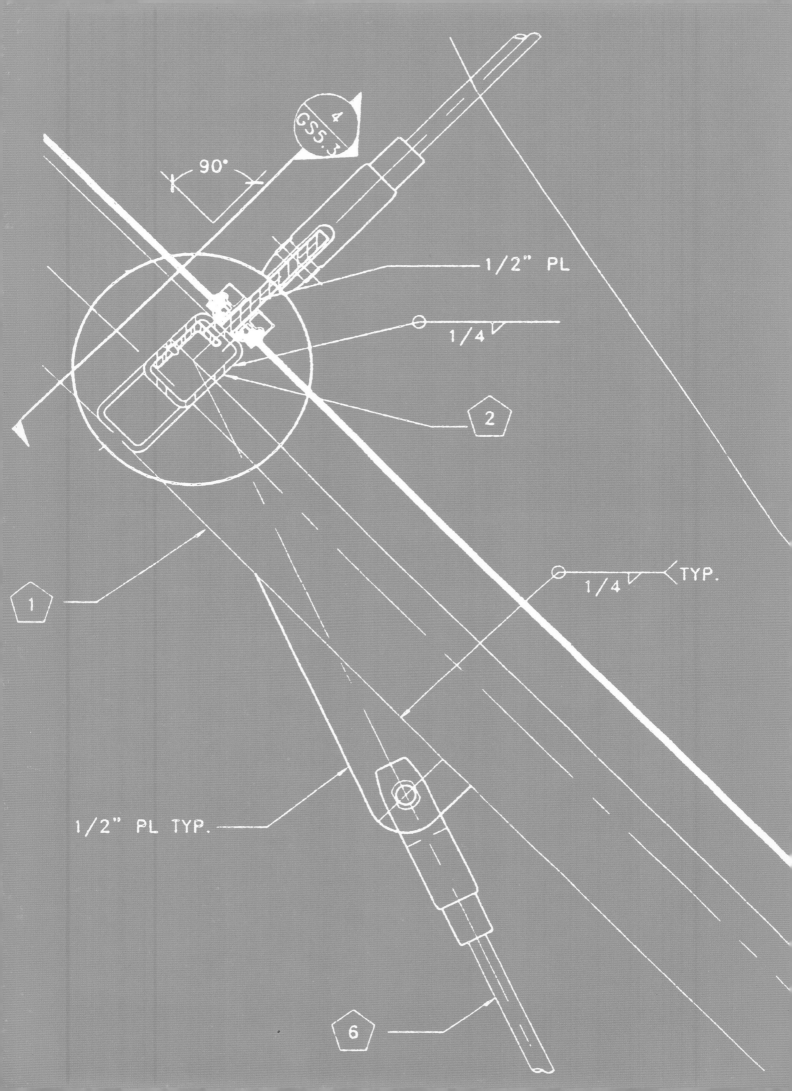

INDEX